Law of Tort

1998–1999 LLB Examination Questions
and Suggested Solutions

University of London
External Examinations

Solutions by Simon Coates, LLB

OLD BAILEY PRESS

OLD BAILEY PRESS
200 Greyhound Road, London W14 9RY

First Published 2001
Reprinted 2001

Examination Questions © The University of London 1998 and 1999

Solutions © The HLT Group Ltd 2001

All Old Bailey Press publications enjoy copyright protection and the copyright belongs to the HLT Group Ltd.

All rights reserved. No part of this publication may be reproduced or transmitted in any form or by any means, electronic, mechanical, photocopying, recording or otherwise, or stored in any retrieval system of any nature without either the written permission of the copyright holder, application for which should be made to the Old Bailey Press, or a licence permitting restricted copying in the United Kingdom issued by the Copyright Licensing Agency.

Any person who infringes the above in relation to this publication may be liable to criminal prosecution and civil claims for damages.

ISBN 1 85836 395 0

British Library Cataloguing-in-Publication.
A CIP Catalogue record for this book is available from the British Library.

Printed and bound in Great Britain

Contents

Acknowledgement	v
Introduction	vii
Examination Paper 1998	3
Suggested Solutions	
Question 1	9
Question 2	13
Question 3	18
Question 4	23
Question 5	28
Question 6	33
Question 7	38
Question 8	43
Examination Paper 1999	49
Suggested Solutions	
Question 1	55
Question 2	61
Question 3	66
Question 4	70
Question 5	74
Question 6	78
Question 7	83
Question 8	87

Acknowledgement

The questions used are taken from the University of London LLB (External) Degree examination papers and our thanks are extended to the University of London for the kind permission which has been given to us to use and publish the questions.

Caveat

The answers given are not approved or sanctioned by the University of London and are entirely our responsibility.

They are not intended as 'Model Answers', but rather as Suggested Solutions.

The answers have two fundamental purposes, namely:

a) to provide a detailed example of a suggested solution to examination questions, and
b) to assist students with their research into the subject and to further their understanding and appreciation of the subject.

Note

Please note that the solutions in this book were written in the year 2000. They were appropriate solutions at the time of preparation, but students must note that certain case law and statutes may subsequently have changed.

Introduction

Why choose Old Bailey Press publications?

In addition to providing students with a comprehensive, accessible range of study materials in the form of our Integrated Student Law Library, Old Bailey Press continues to ensure that students can maximise their potential in examinations with our new series of Suggested Solutions. Our range of Textbooks, 150 Leading Cases, Cracknell's Statute Books and revision aids provide students with an invaluable collection of affordable reference books which will be of assistance from the very beginning of their course right through to the examinations themselves.

Suggested Solutions

The Suggested Solutions series provides examples of full answers to real examination papers. The solutions contained in this book go beyond what would reasonably be expected of a candidate under examination conditions. The opportunity has been taken, where appropriate, to develop themes, suggest alternatives and set out additional material providing further comprehensive topical coverage, making them an excellent addition to the conscientious student's study materials.

We feel that in writing full opinion answers we can assist you with your research and further your understanding and appreciation of the law. It must, however, be recognised that at this level of study there is almost certainly more than only one approach to any examination question.

Notes on examination technique

Although the substance and slant of any answer alters according to the subject-matter of the question, the examining body and the syllabus concerned, the technique required to answer examination questions well does not change.

It is impossible to pass an examination if you do not know the substance of a course. You will only have a slim chance of passing an examination if you have not grasped the technique required for answering a question. In order to do well in your examinations you must learn, and practice, the technique of answering problems correctly. The following is a guide intended to help you acquire that technique.

Time

One of the most daunting aspects of examinations is the imposition of a strict time limit, during which you must answer a set number of questions. Each question will carry a certain number of marks, and it is imperative that you give each question the appropriate period of time for the marks that it carries. It goes without saying that you should not spend an hour answering a 5 mark question and half an hour answering a 20 mark question. If all

Introduction

questions carry equal marks, give them an equal amount of time and attention. Do not be tempted to overrun on a question simply because it is going well.

Reading the question

It will not be often that you will be able to answer every question on an examination paper. Inevitably, there will be some areas in which you feel better prepared than others. You will prefer to answer the questions which deal with those areas, but you will not be able to judge which questions are the best ones for you to answer unless you read the whole examination paper.

You should spend at least ten minutes at the beginning of the examination reading the questions. Preferably, you should read them more than once. As you go through each question, make a brief note on the examination paper of any relevant cases and/or statutes that occur to you even if you think you may not answer that question: you may well be grateful for this note towards the end of the examination when you are tired and your memory begins to fail.

Re-reading the answers

Ideally, you should allow time to re-read your answers. This is rarely a pleasant process, but will ensure that you do not make any silly mistakes such as leaving out a 'not' when the negative is vital. It is very easy to make silly mistakes when writing quickly and under pressure: a re-reading of your answers should help you to spot and correct these errors.

The structure of the answer

Almost all examination problems raise more than one legal issue that you are required to deal with. Your answer should ideally do the following.

Identify the issues raised by the question

This is of crucial importance and gives shape to the whole answer. It indicates to the examiner that you appreciate what he is asking you about.

This is at least as important as actually answering the questions of law raised by that issue. The issues should be identified in the first paragraph of the answer.

Deal with those issues one by one as they arise in the course of the problem

This, of course, is the substance of the answer and where study and revision pay off.

If the answer to an issue turns on a provision of a statute, cite that provision briefly, but do not quote it from any statute you may be permitted to bring into the examination hall

Having cited the provision, show how it is relevant to the question.

If there is no statute, or the meaning of the statute has been interpreted by the courts, cite the relevant cases

'Citing cases' does not mean writing down the name of every case that happens to deal with the general topic with which you are concerned and then detailing all the facts you can think of.

You should cite only the most relevant cases – there may perhaps only be one. No more facts should be stated than are absolutely essential to establish the relevance of the case. If there is a relevant case, but you cannot remember its name, it is sufficient to refer to it as 'one decided case'.

Introduction

Whenever a statute or case is cited, the title of statute or the name of the case should be underlined
This makes the examiner's job much easier because he can see at a glance whether the relevant material has been dealt with, and it will make him more disposed in your favour.

Having dealt with the relevant issues, summarise your conclusions in such a way that you answer the question
A question will often ask you to advise one or more parties. The advice will usually turn on the individual answers to a number of issues. The point made here is that the final paragraph should pull those individual answers together and actually give the advice required. For example, it may begin something like: 'The effect of the answer to the issues raised by this question is that one's advice to A is ...'.

Related to the previous paragraph, make sure at the end that you have answered the question
For example, if the question says 'Advise A', make sure that is what your answer does. If you are required to advise more than one party, make sure that you have dealt with all the parties that you are required to and no more.

Some general points
You should always try to placate the examiner and win him round to your way of thinking. One method has already been mentioned – the underlining of case names, etc. There are also other ways in which you can do this.

Always write as neatly as you can. This is more easily done with ink than with a ball-point. Avoid the use of violently coloured ink eg turquoise; this makes a paper difficult to read. Space out your answers sensibly: leave a line between paragraphs. You can always ask for more paper. At the same time, try not to use so much paper that your answer book looks too formidable to mark. This is a question of personal judgment.

Finally, never put in irrelevant material simply to show that you are clever. Irrelevance is not a virtue, and time spent on it is time lost for other, relevant, answers.

Examination Paper

University of London

LLB Examination June 1998

Law of Tort

Zone A Examination Paper

Time allowed: **three** hours.
Answer **four** of the following **eight** questions.

1. 'The word "nuisance" is difficult to define precisely. It has been said to be protean when questions are raised as to the conduct which may give rise to liability. But the underlying principles, which distinguish the tort of nuisance from the tort of negligence for example, are, I think, capable of reasonably precise definition in the light of the authorities.' (*Hunter* v *Canary Wharf Ltd* (1997), per Lord Hope of Craighead.)
    Discuss.

2. Juliet is a doctor who works for the Laburnam Street Surgery, a National Health Service practice in an inner-city area. Because there have been several attacks on doctors on night call, the practice has an arrangement with Owlish Security Services to provide a guard to drive the doctor's car. Juliet is called out one night to a patient living in a large block of flats. She went into the flats leaving Dale, a guard from the security firm, sitting in the driver's seat. Two men attacked the car. One of them distracted Dale's attention by trying to open the back door. While Dale dealt with him, the other opened the passenger door, removed a pad of prescription forms which Juliet had left in the glove compartment and ran off. Juliet did not discover the loss until the next day. Meanwhile the thieves had given some prescription forms to their friends, one of whom, Liam, used a form to obtain a supply of drugs from a pharmacy. Liam suffered permanent brain damage as a result of taking the drugs.
    Advise Liam's father.

3. Every month a national newspaper The Clarion publishes the serial numbers of premium bonds which have won large prizes in that month's draw. Louisa read the list one month, checked her numbers and saw that one of her bonds had won a prize of £100,000. A week earlier in her public library she had been reading a copy of The Dabbler, a weekly periodical which gives investment advice. She remembered readers being advised to consider purchasing shares as soon as possible in Dentache plc, whose research scientists were said to be on the brink of a revolutionary new technique for arresting tooth decay. This information was seriously misleading and The Dabbler published a correction in the next issue, but Louisa had not read this. Louisa

Law of Tort – June 1998

immediately decided to invest a large part of her prize money in Dentache plc and purchased shares to the value of £80,000.

In the list of prizewinners in The Clarion two digits had been transposed incorrectly and Louisa had not won a prize. The shares in Dentache plc have not risen in value. They fell slightly after she purchased them, but have now risen to the price at which she purchased them.

Advise Louisa.

4. Belinda went to Mugshots, a firm of photographers, to obtain passport photographs. She was accompanied by her six-year-old son Craig, who is very deaf. Mugshots was having new shelving installed by Derek in a room adjoining the waiting area. Derek worked for the local council, but was doing the work for Mugshots in his own time in the evenings and at weekends. There was a swing door through from the waiting area to the area where Derek was working. Belinda was called into the booth to have her photographs taken, and told Craig to wait reading his comic. Craig however wandered off and pushed the swing doors. Ethel, the receptionist, shouted to him to come back, but he did not hear and went through the door. Derek had left a stepladder leaning against some half-finished shelving. Craig knocked against the ladder. The shelving fell on him, causing him a broken arm and leg. Belinda went running to him when she heard his screams. She has suffered from severe depression since the incident.

Advise Belinda and Craig.

5. 'Causation in tort should be a matter of common sense and not of philosophical theory.'
Discuss.

6. Richard worked as a gardener with the Peony District Council. He was planting out a bed of rose bushes which the council had purchased from the Floribunda Nurseries. The bushes had been treated with a spray to repel greenfly. It is known that a number of people react to the spray for some days after it has been applied. Richard began to feel breathless, but, before anyone could come to his assistance, he had collapsed. It appears that he is abnormally allergic to the spray. He has suffered permanent brain damage. He is happy and in no physical pain but is unable to look after himself, to work or to pursue his hobby of darts. His mother Stella has given up her job in a supermarket to look after him, but she is quite elderly and it is expected that Richard will eventually have to go into a home.

Advise Richard (a) as to any claims he may have in tort and (b) as to the assessment of damages.

7. Chill and Douche, two members of the building inspections team in the Loamshire Fire Brigade, carried out an inspection of the engineering building at Loamshire University. They reported that the notice boards were a fire hazard and that, if notices continued to be displayed anywhere in the corridors and staircases other than in specially constructed glass cases, they would seek a court order closing the building. At a meeting with student representatives a few days later, Flame, the Dean of Engineering, remarked that because of 'the Hitlerite tendency' of the local fire brigade, he had to prohibit students from displaying any notices advertising their societies. The next issue of the Student

Union newspaper carried a banner headline reading, '"FIRE INSPECTORS ARE FASCIST SCUM", SAYS DEAN.' Copies of this newspaper are handed out to students on the campus, and are also prominently on sale in local newsagents.

Advise the parties as to any possible claims in defamation.

8. a) Discuss the concept of necessity as a defence to an action in trespasss.
   b) Hilda enters hospital for major abdominal surgery. Ingrid, the surgical registrar, describes the nature of the operation to her and she signs a form consenting to the surgery. During the operation Ingrid notices that Hilda's appendix is diseased and is likely to cause her serious problems in a year or two. She therefore removes it. Hilda is annoyed when she discovers that this has happened.

   Advise her.

Suggested Solutions

Question One

'The word "nuisance" is difficult to define precisely. It has been said to be protean when questions are raised as to the conduct which may give rise to liability. But the underlying principles, which distinguish the tort of nuisance from the tort of negligence for example, are, I think, capable of reasonably precise definition in the light of the authorities.' (*Hunter* v *Canary Wharf Ltd* (1997), per Lord Hope of Craighead.)

Discuss.

Suggested Solution

General Comment

Recent developments in tort are always likely to form the basis of examination questions, especially important decisions of the House of Lords. Those candidates who had carefully studied the judgment in *Hunter* and its wider implications would have been well placed to answer this question. As ever, a more detailed analysis and comment on the case was expected of candidates, as a compromise to predictability.

Skeleton Solution

Introduce the tort of private nuisance in relation to the *Hunter* case – describe why the tort may be said to be 'protean' in nature, given its application to a wide range of scenarios – what are the distinguishing features of nuisance and negligence (as identified by their Lordships)? – why were these important in the *Hunter* case? – describe the court's decision regarding standing, damages and the applicability of the tort to interference with TV reception (including Lord Cooke's dissent) – conclude by saying something about the importance of the decision in *Hunter* and possible future activity in this area.

Suggested Solution

The case of *Hunter and Others* v *Canary Wharf Limited* (1) raised important questions as to the scope of the tort of private nuisance. The tort itself is concerned with unreasonable interference with a person's use or enjoyment of his land, or some right over or in connection with his land. The House of Lords in *Hunter* explained the tort as falling within three main categories: nuisance by encroachment on a neighbour's land; nuisance by direct physical injury to a neighbour's land; and nuisance by interference with a neighbour's quiet enjoyment of his land.

These categories are extremely wide in that they cover a large variety of potential claims and factual scenarios. For example, under the third category, interference might be caused by dirt, dust, noise, smoke, smell and vibrations arising from a huge range of activites. In *Thompson-Schwab v Costaki* (2) the sight of prostitutes and their clients entering and leaving neighbouring premises amounted to a private nuisance. In *Khorasandjian v Bush* (3) the Court of Appeal even went so far as to grant an injunction in favour of a young girl against the defendant, who had embarked on a course of harassment against her at the parental home. In *Hunter*, one of the questions before the Lords was whether interference with TV reception suffered by local residents following the construction of the Canary Wharf tower (a building which is almost 250 metres high, over 50 metres square, and clad in stainless steel) could amount to a private nuisance. A second, more fundamental, question related to who had the right to bring an action in nuisance for the interference caused to TV reception, and, in a separate action, for dust caused by the construction of a link road to the Docklands area.

It was this question which prompted the majority of the Lords to comment upon the distinguishing features of actions in nuisance and negligence, and it is this aspect of the *Hunter* case which will be dealt with first.

The distinguishing factors of negligence and nuisance
Lord Hoffmann, quoting from Lord Simonds in *Read v Lyons Ltd* (4), noted that nuisance only protects interests in land, and that it is a tort of strict liability ie it is no defence for a defendant to say that he took all reasonable steps to prevent it. Negligence, on the other hand, is fault-based (breach of a duty to take reasonable care) and protects interests of many kinds, not just those in land. Lord Cooke noted that in nuisance, damages may be recovered for interference with the use and enjoyment of land, whereas there is no remedy for discomfort or distress (not resulting in bodily or psychiatric injury) in negligence. Lord Hope, in examining the scope of each tort, noted that the function of nuisance is to control the activities of an owner/occupier of property within the boundaries of his own land which may harm the owner/occupier of neighbouring land. In other words, the duty is owed to owners and occupiers. In negligence, however, the duty extends to those who are foreseeably closely and directly affected by the defendant's act or omission: *Donoghue v Stevenson* (5). In appropriate circumstances, this might include persons on neighbouring land who are neither owners nor occupiers. It should be noted that in some situations, the two torts overlap and may provide concurrent remedies.

The right to sue in private nuisance
The decision of the majority flowed from the proposition that nuisance is a tort which attaches to land ie is directed against the claimant's enjoyment of the land affected. On this basis, an action in nuisance can only be brought by a person who has an interest in such land. These persons might include one who has actual possession, such as a freeholder, tenant in possession or a licensee with exclusive possession, or a reversioner, where the nuisance is sufficiently permanent in character to damage the reversion itself.

The Lords impliedly accepted the decision of the Court of Appeal in *Foster v Warblington UDC* (6) which upheld the right, in exceptional cases, of someone who has exclusive possession of land (even though he cannot prove title) to sue in private nuisance. Lord Lloyd stated that the first two categories of private nuisance involve damage to land and therefore only a person who has a proprietary interest in that land can sue. By implication, therefore this must also be true of the third category. Lord Hoffmann agreed that the third category did not constitute a separate tort.

In a powerful dissent, Lord Cooke argued that whilst the decision of the majority achieves symmetry and uniformity in the law of nuisance (the rules being the same for each of the three categories), their approach does not give adequate weight to current perceptions of the rights and status of spouses, de facto partners and children living at home. In relation to children in particular, he noted the recognition given to the interests of children by international convention. Article 16 of the UN Convention on the Rights of the Child protects children from unlawful interference with their home. Article 8 of the European Convention for the Protection of Human Rights and Fundamental Freedoms recognises the right to respect for private and family life, aimed in part at protecting the home. Jurisprudence of the European Court of Human Rights shows that the protection of the home extends to protection from nuisance, even though children clearly have no proprietary rights over the family home.

Lord Cooke therefore considered the Court of Appeal decision of *Khorasandjian* to have been correctly decided and regarded the fact of 'occupation of property as a home' to be an acceptable basis from which to bring an action in nuisance. He felt that other resident members of the family, de facto partners and lodgers, could as a matter of policy be allowed to claim in private nuisance if they had suffered a 'truly serious interference with domestic amenities'.

However, the majority of their Lordships overruled *Khorasandjian*, Lords Goff and Lloyd stating that the Court of Appeal had simply exploited the tort of nuisance in order to introduce, by the back door, a tort of harassment out of sympathy with the claimant. They noted that a tort of harassment had since received statutory protection under the Protection from Harassment Act 1997, and a remedy was no longer needed at common law. The approach taken in *Khorasandjian* was to transform the tort of nuisance to one which attaches to the person rather than to land. The effect would be to allow a claimant to recover for loss less severe than personal injury upon criteria relating only to the balancing of the interests of neighbours, rather than negligence.

Damages
The proposition that the tort of nuisance attaches to land only also formed the basis of the decision of the majority as to the correct measure of damages recoverable in nuisance. Under the first two categories of nuisance involving damage to land, compensation will be assessed according to the diminution in value of the property. This will normally be the cost of remedial work and repair. However, where a nuisance simply affects the enjoyment of land, then damages will be assessed according to the loss of the amenity value of the land, assuming the nuisance does not affect the overall market value. This would be a relatively low single payment to the proprietor(s) of the land, and will not depend upon the overall number of people who were affected.

Although not necessary for the actual decision in *Hunter*, considerable doubt was cast upon the question of whether damages for personal injury are recoverable in private nuisance. Lord Goff stated that the correct action for the recovery of such loss is negligence. Lord Hoffmann drew attention to the anomalous outcome of compensation for personal injury being easier to recover if suffered at home rather than at work.

TV reception

It was agreed unanimously that interference to TV reception in the circumstances did not amount to a private nuisance. The Lords held that a building, which by its mere presence prevents something from reaching the claimant's land, is not a nuisance. The tort must take the form of something emanating from the defendant's land, or, occasionally, from some offensive conduct of neighbours. The blocking of TV reception was comparable by analogy with the loss of a view, which is not actionable in private nuisance. Lords Goff and Hoffmann agreed that at common law, people are entitled to build freely on their land unless restricted by a covenant or an easement. It was further doubted whether an easement could exist against the interruption of TV/radio signals.

A common theme of the majority of their Lordships' judgments related to the unpredictability of building developments causing interference with TV reception, and the large number of potential claimants involved in such a situation. Lords Goff and Hoffmann pointed out that the most appropriate time to raise an objection to possible TV interference would have been at the stage of application for planning permission to the local planning authority, although it was noted that this course of action would not have been open to the residents in this case. Lord Cooke preferred to approach the question according to the reasonable user test, holding that Canary Wharf Tower had been a reasonable development in all the circumstances.

Conclusion

The decision in *Hunter* is an important one, because it preserves the distinction between nuisance and negligence as two separate torts subject to different rules. It settled the question of who can sue in private nuisance and the basis for awarding damages for loss of the use and enjoyment of land. It might be argued that Lord Cooke's approach to the question of standing should achieve favour in the future, as the courts are now under an obligation to decide a case's compatibility with Convention rights (unless prevented from doing so by primary legislation), and to take into account the jurisprudence of the European Court of Human Rights in doing so: Human Rights Act 1998. The protection of the home, as an aspect of the right to respect for private and family life, contained in art 8 of the Convention, seems to require protection to be given to all members of the household against nuisances.

Important questions have yet to be answered following *Hunter*; for example, whether damages for personal injury are available in nuisance and whether interference with TV reception caused by something emanating from the defendant's land can form the basis of an action. Further judicial activity in this area can be anticipated. For the time being, the House of Lords appear to have applied the brakes to the development of the tort of nuisance to cover novel situations.

References

(1) [1997] 2 All ER 426
(2) [1956] 1 WLR 335
(3) [1993] 3 WLR 476
(4) [1947] AC 156
(5) [1932] AC 562
(6) [1906] 1 KB 648

Question Two

Juliet is a doctor who works for the Laburnam Street Surgery, a National Health Service practice in an inner-city area. Because there have been several attacks on doctors on night call, the practice has an arrangement with Owlish Security Services to provide a guard to drive the doctor's car. Juliet is called out one night to a patient living in a large block of flats. She went into the flats leaving Dale, a guard from the security firm, sitting in the driver's seat. Two men attacked the car. One of them distracted Dale's attention by trying to open the back door. While Dale dealt with him, the other opened the passenger door, removed a pad of prescription forms which Juliet had left in the glove compartment and ran off. Juliet did not discover the loss until the next day. Meanwhile the thieves had given some prescription forms to their friends, one of whom, Liam, used a form to obtain a supply of drugs from a pharmacy. Liam suffered permanent brain damage as a result of taking the drugs.

Advise Liam's father.

Suggested Solution

General Comment

This would have proved a popular question for candidates involving, as it did, consideration of the elements of the tort of negligence. Candidates should have appreciated that this was not a question concerning the duty of care owed by doctors to their patients. An analysis of the current authorities involving possible duties to prevent harm arising from the deliberate wrongful acts of third parties was required. Much of the discussion should have centred around the existence or otherwise of a duty of care, and related issues of causation and remoteness.

Skeleton Solution

Primary liability of Juliet – did she owe a duty to safeguard the prescription forms to prevent them from falling into the wrong hands? – was there a breach of duty? – did the intervening criminal conduct of the thieves and/or Liam's own decision to use the prescription to obtain the drugs amount to a novus actus interveniens? – was Liam contributory negligent? – was Dale also liable in negligence (on similar grounds)? – vicarious liability – were the partners of the surgery liable for Juliet's wrongdoing? – if Dale was negligent, who was his employer?

Law of Tort – June 1998

Suggested Solution

Primary liability of Juliet

The issue here is whether Juliet could be said to owe a duty to safeguard property in her control so that it could not be used to injure others. The establishment of such a duty of care, together with the further issue of whether, in law, Juliet could be said to have caused Liam's injuries, are fraught with difficulty.

Duty of care

Following the case of *Caparo Industries Ltd plc* v *Dickman* (1) there is now a three-stage test in order to determine whether a duty of care arises in a novel situation.

1. The harm suffered by Liam must have been reasonably foreseeable. It is submitted that there is no great problem with this test. A reasonable person would surely have foreseen that the blank prescriptions might be the subject of a theft in an inner city area in which the incidence of crime necessitated the hiring of a security guard. It must also have been reasonably foreseeable that stolen prescriptions would inevitably fall into the wrong hands and be used to obtain supplies of drugs, the dangerous consequences of which are obvious.

2. There must have been a relationship of proximity between Juliet and Liam. The application of this test is far more problematic. There is no pre-existing relationship between Juliet and Liam. In addition, this is a case of non-feasance on the part of Juliet, ie a failure to safeguard property in her control so as to prevent it from falling into the wrong hands. It is unlikely that any positive duty to look after the prescription forms arises unless, possibly, she has been issued with guidelines as to their security. In the case of non-feasance, duties to prevent harm arising from the deliberate wrongful acts of third parties are only created in exceptional circumstances. There is no general common law duty to this effect.

    Lord Goff, in *Smith* v *Littlewoods Organisation Ltd* (2), identified four situations in which such an exceptional duty might arise (although he conceded that there might be others) the most analogous of which are as follows.

    a) Where there is a special relationship between the defendant and the third parties who inflict damage by criminal activity. Such a duty was held to exist in *Home Office* v *Dorset Yacht Co Ltd* (3) in which damage done by escaped inmates of a Borstal institution was held to be recoverable, the escape arising from the negligent supervision of the inmates by three Borstal officers. However, a special relationship only arose in that case as a result of the statutory duties placed on Borstal authorities to control their trainees. In this case Juliet clearly has no responsibility in respect of the two men who attacked the car, and therefore it is submitted that no liability arises for their wrongful act under this exception.

    b) Where the defendant knows, or has the means to know, that a third party is creating a danger on his property and he fails to take reasonable steps to abate the danger. Thus in *Smith*, the defendants were not held liable in respect of their failure to prevent vandals from entering their unoccupied premises and starting a fire which spread to the plaintiff's property. Although their Lordships conceded that there is a general duty on occupiers to ensure that their premises are not a source of danger to neighbouring properties, this did not extend to preventing vandals from doing damage where a reasonable person would not have foreseen that steps were necessary to make the premises lockfast. In *Smith*, a reasonable person in the defendant's position would not have foreseen the need to secure the premises, as the defendant had no notice that vagrants were regularly in the building or that fires had previously been started there.

Lord Goff's approach was subsequently followed by the Court of Appeal in *Topp* v *London Country Bus (South West) Ltd* (4) in which the defendant was held not to be liable for a hit and run incident caused by joyriders who stole the defendant's minibus, even though the vehicle had been left unlocked with the key in the ignition awaiting a relief driver. It could be argued that, since Juliet knew of the high incidence of attacks on doctors in the area, she failed to take reasonable steps to abate the danger, especially if the previous attacks were with a view to obtaining blank prescriptions. She might, for example, have taken a smaller number of prescription forms with her rather than a whole pad, and taken some extra steps to secure them, such as locking them away in the glove compartment or in the boot of the car.

3. It must be fair, just and reasonable for the court to impose a duty of care in all the circumstances of the case. This is, of course, difficult to assess. The court might be persuaded to extend the duty recognised in *Smith* to Juliet's circumstances as the facts are clearly analogous. Such an incremental development would not appear to fall foul of policy considerations, such as the need to prevent a flood of possible similar claims.

Breach
The factors relevant to whether Juliet's conduct fell below that to be expected of the reasonable person have been discussed above, when considering whether she failed to take reasonable steps to abate the danger.

Causation and remoteness
There is no doubt that Juliet's failure to safeguard the prescription forms was a factual cause of Liam's injuries. There is, however, a major issue as to whether, as a matter of law, she should be held liable for the damage which she has in fact caused. There are two possible intervening events (novus actus interveniens) which may serve to break the link between Juliet's possible negligence and Liam's injuries.

1. The intervening criminal conduct of the two men who stole the prescription forms. In *Home Office* v *Dorset Yacht Co Ltd* Lord Reid stated:

    'Where human action forms one of the links between the original wrongdoing and the loss suffered by the plaintiff, the action must at least have been something very likely to occur if not to be regarded as a novus actus interveniens.'

This proposition is clearly closely related to the question of whether Juliet owed a duty to take reasonable steps to prevent the possibility of a theft, given her knowledge of the likelihood of attacks in the area. It is submitted that if Juliet owes a duty to Liam similar to that which was identified in *Smith*, then the damage caused by the third parties will

not be regarded as too remote a consequence of a breach of that duty. The issues of duty, causation and remoteness are closely linked in situations such as these.
2. The intervening decision of Liam to use the stolen prescription form in order to obtain a supply of drugs. The unreasonable intervening conduct (going beyond a matter of pure contributory negligence) of the claimant will amount to a novus actus interveniens: *McKew v Holland & Hannen & Cubitts (Scotland) Ltd* (5). It is submitted that Liam's actions fall well within the scope of this rule, and his loss will therefore be treated as too remote from any negligence on the part of Juliet to warrant recovery.

Defences
In the unlikely event that Juliet were to be held liable for Liam's injuries, Liam's damages would undoubtedly be substantially reduced having regard to his share in the responsibility for the loss: s1(1) Law Reform (Contributory Negligence) Act 1945. Clearly Liam was very much at fault in using the stolen prescription to obtain the drugs and in subsequently consuming them.

Primary liability of Dale
The basis for the possible liability of Dale will be very similar to that of Juliet, although some differences apply. It is submitted that a duty to safeguard property left in his control will only arise if Dale was aware of the presence of the prescription forms in the glove compartment. The fact that Dale remained in the car might indicate that Juliet had left him there for the purpose of guarding the forms rather than to provide personal protection for her upon entering the block of flats. On the other hand, the lapse in time before discovering that the forms had gone missing might indicate that Dale's attention hadn't been drawn to the presence of the forms in the first place.

If one of Dale's functions was to safeguard the prescription forms, then his failure to lock the passenger door whilst waiting in this particular neighbourhood would be an additional factor suggesting a breach of duty.

Vicarious liability
If Juliet has been negligent in failing to safeguard the forms, then the other partners in the Laburnam Street Surgery will liable to the same extent under the Partnership Act 1890.

Dale's employer will also be vicariously liable for any negligence on his part. The fact that he may have been discharging his duties in a negligent or careless manner will not take him outside the course of his employment: *Century Insurance Co v Northern Ireland Road Transport Board* (6). The only question remaining is whether Dale is an employee of Owlish Security Services, the agency which supplied him, or of the Laburnum Street Surgery. The modern approach is for the courts to consider a range of factors in relation to each potential employer such as:

1. who provided Dale's wage or other remuneration;
2. who paid his national insurance contributions;
3. who directed Dale as to the mode of performance of his work to such a degree as to make the other his employer;
4. who had the power to dismiss Dale; and
5. how long has Dale worked for the Laburnum Street Surgery?

There is little evidence in the question as to Dale's true position, although the fact that he drives the doctor's car, rather than one supplied by Owlish Security, is some indication that he may be an employee of the surgery.

References

(1) [1990] 2 AC 605
(2) [1987] AC 241
(3) [1970] AC 1004
(4) [1993] 3 All ER 448
(5) [1969] 3 All ER 1621
(6) [1942] AC 509

Question Three

Every month a national newspaper The Clarion publishes the serial numbers of premium bonds which have won large prizes in that month's draw. Louisa read the list one month, checked her numbers and saw that one of her bonds had won a prize of £100,000. A week earlier in her public library she had been reading a copy of The Dabbler, a weekly periodical which gives investment advice. She remembered readers being advised to consider purchasing shares as soon as possible in Dentache plc, whose research scientists were said to be on the brink of a revolutionary new technique for arresting tooth decay. This information was seriously misleading and The Dabbler published a correction in the next issue, but Louisa had not read this. Louisa immediately decided to invest a large part of her prize money in Dentache plc and purchased shares to the value of £80,000.

In the list of prizewinners in The Clarion two digits had been transposed incorrectly and Louisa had not won a prize. The shares in Dentache plc have not risen in value. They fell slightly after she purchased them, but have now risen to the price at which she purchased them.

Advise Louisa.

Suggested Solution

General Comment

This question required more thought, and possibly a more detailed analysis of the facts, than was the case with the other problem questions on this paper. Candidates needed to know the rules necessary to impose liability for economic loss caused by negligent advice and information, and had to be able to apply them to a set of rather awkward facts. Different approaches to structure were also possible here. Candidates should have made some observations about the different economic losses that arose in this case, and whether they were all recoverable, bearing in mind the general aim of damages in tort. Such discussion would normally be reserved until the end of a question. However, candidates could have set the scene by making it clear from the outset which losses Louisa might have been able to recover (if at all).

Skeleton Solution

Identify, in relation to the aims of damages in tort, which losses Louisa might be able to recover following her reliance on negligent information and advice – discuss whether Louisa was owed a duty of care by The Dabbler in respect of economic losses caused by reliance on negligent investment advice (investigate whether a 'special relationship' existed between

Law of Tort – June 1998

them and whether Louisa reasonably relied on their advice) – discuss whether Louisa was owed a duty of care by The Clarion in respect of economic losses caused by reliance on negligently provided information.

Suggested Solution

This question concerns potential liability for economic loss caused by negligent advice and information. It is more difficult to impose liability for negligent statements than for negligent actions: careless words can spread rapidly resulting in a proliferation of claims and potentially unlimited financial losses. Therefore, policy considerations have led to the introduction of rules which limit the class of potential claimants in such cases. The mere foresight of harm arising from negligent advice is insufficient to establish a duty of care.

Which losses might Louisa be able to recover in negligent misstatement?
It should be noted from the outset that, even if duties of care can be established in this case, Louisa is unlikely to be able to claim for all the potential losses she has suffered. This is because the aim of damages in tort is to restore the claimant to the position she would have been in had the tort never been committed (the 'reliance' interest). There have been very few tort cases in which the claim resulted in an award of damages to protect the 'expectation' interest, ie by putting the claimant into the position she would have been in had the defendant properly carried out their obligation. One exceptional category of cases have arisen in relation to the negligent execution of a testator's instructions by a solicitor in the preparation of a will: see *Ross v Caunters* (1) and *White v Jones* (2). However, these cases appear to represent a very limited exception to the general rule.

The losses accruing to Louisa in this case seem to be as follows.

1. The loss of interest/investment income on the £80,000 which Louisa would have earned had she not withdrawn the funds to invest in Dentache plc shares.
2. The administration costs of buying (and possibly selling) the shares.
3. Any loss resulting from a fall in the value of Dentache plc shares. It should be noted that Louisa has not actually made a loss, since the price of these shares has recovered, and it is submitted that she may now be under a duty to mitigate her loss by selling the shares in order to prevent future loss from accruing (assuming she is to claim in negligent misstatement).
4. The failure to make an economic gain, ie a profit from the Dentache plc shares, which would have been made had the information quoted in The Dabbler been correct.

The loss in (4) above clearly relates to the expectation interest, and is not recoverable in negligent misstatement. The restoration of Louisa to the position she was in before any tort took place would require the courts to ensure that Louisa had suffered neither financial loss nor financial gain. It is submitted that it would not be fair, just and reasonable to expect the maker of a statement to be held responsible for a lack of financial gain arising from negligent advice. As a matter of policy, it might be thought that those who 'gamble' in the hope of making a profit should be expected to accept the risk of making a loss.

Law of Tort – June 1998

Is Louisa owed a duty of care by The Dabbler in respect of the (pure) economic losses arising from the negligent investment advice?
The development of this area of law has been heavily influenced by trends in judicial policy and therefore the decisions have not always been consistent. However, some common requirements can be deduced from the body of case law, starting with the House of Lord's decision in *Hedley Byrne & Co Ltd v Heller & Partners Ltd* (3).

A duty of care arising from a negligent misstatement can only be established if the following two criteria apply.

1. There must have been a special relationship (of close proximity) between the claimant and the defendant.

    The existence of such a relationship is dependent upon a variety of factors. It has been suggested that a relationship 'equivalent to contract' must exist between the claimant and defendant before the defendant will be held to have voluntarily assumed responsibility to the claimant. See the judgements of Lord Devlin in *Hedley Byrne* and Lord Templeman in *Smith v Eric S Bush (A Firm)* (4). In the instant case, it could be argued that such a relationship might exist between The Dabbler and those who purchase copies of it from a retailer. Whether such a relationship could be said to exist in respect of those who simply read the magazine in a public library is more difficult to say. In *Caparo Industries Ltd plc v Dickman* (5), Lord Oliver defined the range of persons to whom a duty is owed in terms of the purpose for which the statement was made. He identified four necessary elements for the existence of a duty of care, as explained below.

    a) The advice must be required for a purpose which is either specified in detail or described in general terms, and this purpose must be expressly or inferentially made known to the advisor when the advice is given.

        The whole purpose of The Dabbler is to give investment advice to its readership, and this would of course have been known to the editorial staff. However, whether the purpose is simply to give general investment advice (to point readers in the right direction) or to give specific information about companies is unclear. It could be argued that the information concerning Dentache plc was very specific, and the fact that the magazine advised its readers to consider purchasing shares 'as soon as possible' might indicate that The Dabbler had voluntarily assumed responsibility to their readership in respect of the accuracy of this information.

        On the other hand, it could be argued that the advice being given was simply to 'consider' purchasing shares in Dentache plc, and therefore the purpose was to suggest that readers might make an investment after undertaking further research and possibly obtaining a second opinion. It must be remembered that the rules, as a matter of policy, are intended to reduce the potential class of claimants. The losses accruing to The Dabbler and other similar periodicals would potentially be unlimited if every reader were permitted to recover for financial losses following reliance on poor investment advice. In *James McNaughten Paper Group plc v Hicks Anderson & Co (A Firm)* (6) Neill LJ identified, as an additional relevant factor, the size of any class of persons to which the advisee belongs. It is submitted that it is unlikely that the courts would impose a duty of care on The Dabbler in respect of the advice honestly given, as the potential class of claimants would be very large.

b) The advisor must know (expressly or inferentially) that the advice will be communicated to the claimant, either specifically or to a member of an ascertained class, in order that it should be used by the advisee for that purpose. It is submitted that The Dabbler must be aware that its potential readers are likely to include those who visit public libraries.

c) It must be expressly or inferentially known that the advice communicated is likely to be acted upon by the advisee for that purpose without independent enquiry (see below on 'reasonable' reliance).

d) The advice must be acted upon by the advisee to his detriment.

The advice given must be formal considered advice. 'Off the cuff' advice or 'passing comment' will not usually give rise to a special relationship. However, it is submitted that written advice contained in a magazine whose purpose it is to inform its readership of investment decisions must be regarded as formal considered advice. The person giving the advice must usually possess some special skill/knowledge: *Esso Petroleum Co Ltd* v *Mardon* (7). It can be assumed that those who write for The Dabbler have some expertise in the field of investment decisions, or at least hold themselves out as doing so.

2. It must have been reasonable for the claimant to rely on the defendant's statement.

Louisa clearly relied on the advice she had read, as she was influenced to invest on the strength of it. It is unlikely, however, that her reliance was reasonable. It has already been pointed out that the purpose of such a magazine might only have been to inform general investment decision-making by pointing readers in the right direction. It would seem unreasonable for Louisa to make such a large investment without undertaking further research or even seeking independent financial advice. This is particularly the case given that Louisa's decision was based upon her recollection of an article in a magazine which was published a week earlier. The price of shares in Dentache plc might already have increased following the earlier publicity and the investment might no longer be regarded as a good one.

It is submitted, therefore, that Louisa is not owed a duty of care by The Dabbler in respect of the advice given, in that no special relationship arose between them (the advice arguably not having been provided for the purpose of making specific investment decisions) and in any event, it would have been unreasonable for Louisa to rely on the advice in the circumstances.

Even if a duty was owed by The Dabbler to its readers, it could be argued that the duty was discharged by the printing of a correction in the first available issue, at least in respect of losses sustained after publication.

Is Louisa owed a duty of care by The Clarion in respect of the misprint?

The failure to correctly transpose the serial numbers of the winning premium bonds also gives rise to difficulty. In applying the criteria identified by Lord Oliver in *Caparo* it seems likely that a special relationship did arise between The Clarion and Louisa. The newspaper knew that the information they gave would be used by readers for the purpose of checking their serial numbers. It is also clear that Louisa relied on this information to her detriment.

However, the main issue is whether it can be said that Louisa reasonably relied on the printed information. Surely the newspaper could reasonably expect Louisa to receive official confirmation of her win, or at least to confirm the numbers from another source, before relying on the information. There is also some authority to suggest that the courts may draw a distinction between the mere passing on of information and the giving of advice based upon that information: see the Privy Council case of *Royal Bank Trust Co (Trinidad) Ltd v Pampellonne* (8). The mere printing of winning serial numbers might simply be regarded as the passing on of information, and therefore, would not give rise to any duty of care.

References

(1)   [1980] Ch 297
(2)   [1995] 2 WLR 187
(3)   [1964] AC 465
(4)   [1990] 1 AC 831
(5)   [1990] 2 AC 605
(6)   [1991] 1 All ER 134
(7)   [1976] 1 QB 801
(8)   [1987] 1 Lloyd's Rep 218

Question Four

Belinda went to Mugshots, a firm of photographers, to obtain passport photographs. She was accompanied by her six-year-old son Craig, who is very deaf. Mugshots was having new shelving installed by Derek in a room adjoining the waiting area. Derek worked for the local council, but was doing the work for Mugshots in his own time in the evenings and at weekends. There was a swing door through from the waiting area to the area where Derek was working. Belinda was called into the booth to have her photographs taken, and told Craig to wait reading his comic. Craig however wandered off and pushed the swing doors. Ethel, the receptionist, shouted to him to come back, but he did not hear and went through the door. Derek had left a stepladder leaning against some half-finished shelving. Craig knocked against the ladder. The shelving fell on him, causing him a broken arm and leg. Belinda went running to him when she heard his screams. She has suffered from severe depression since the incident.

Advise Belinda and Craig.

Suggested Solution

General Comment

This is a question involving loss or injury to someone who comes onto another person's premises, resulting from a defect in the premises. Any such case should be dealt with as a statutory claim under the Occupiers' Liability Acts, rather than in common law negligence. The suggested solution given below is a very full answer to this question, and in an examination it would be permissible to deal only very briefly with the elements of occupiers' liability which are not really in issue eg 'occupier', 'premises' and Craig's status as a visitor.

Skeleton Solution

Explain and identify the 'occupier' of the premises concerned – discuss whether Craig is a visitor or trespasser when he enters the room adjacent to the waiting area – identify the relevant Occupiers' Liability Act – discuss whether the occupier owed Craig a duty of care, and if so, whether such a duty was broken – did Mugshots discharge their duty to Craig by providing a sufficient warning, or by the proper selection and supervision of an independent contractor? – can Belinda claim for her 'nervous shock' as a secondary victim of the accident?

Suggested Solution

The question concerns the liability of an occupier of premises for damage done to those who come onto the premises. The law relating to such liability is largely to be found in the Occupiers' Liability Act (OLA) 1957 as regards visitors to premises.

The occupier of the premises
Under s1(2) OLA 1957 the definition of 'occupier' remains the same as at common law. In this scenario, the occupier of the building in which the accident occurred is clearly Mugshots, as it is they who had a 'sufficient degree of control over the premises' and 'ought to have realised that any failure on their part to use care may result in injury': *Wheat* v *E Lacon and Co Ltd* (1).

However, it is possible for there to be more than one occupier of premises at the same time. Multiple occupation was contemplated as a possibility by Lord Denning in *Wheat* (above) and was held to exist in *AMF International Ltd* v *Magnet Bowling Ltd* (2). The question may arise as to whether Derek could be regarded as an occupier of the room adjoining the waiting area: even though he is not present during normal opening hours, he presumably has some ongoing control over the work area and the state in which it is left. Whilst every case turns upon its own facts, it was held in *Page* v *Read* (3) that the degree of control associated with the presence and activities of a decorator painting a house was insufficient to give rise to a duty as an occupier. It is therefore submitted that the sole occupier(s) of the business premises in this scenario are likely to be the partners of Mugshots.

This does not prevent Derek from being held liable for Craig's injuries as a non-occupier under ordinary negligence principles, and it has been noted that there is little difference between the standards of care required in ordinary common law negligence compared to those required under OLA 1957. However, ultimately Craig would be best advised to pursue the defendant with the deepest pockets, and this will require a claim against Mugshots under OLA 1957, who are the most likely defendant to carry public liability insurance.

Premises
The room adjacent to the waiting area and the shelving are clearly premises within the meaning of OLA 1957, with s1(3)(a) of the Act referring to 'any fixed or moveable structure'. Even a ladder could be regarded as 'premises' provided it remains in control of the occupier when the accident occurs: *Wheeler* v *Copas* (4).

Is Craig a visitor or trespasser?
Section 1(2) OLA 1957 states that a lawful visitor is, for the purposes of the Act, either an invitee or a licensee. This requires such a person to have had the occupier's express or implied permission to come on to the premises. Craig is a visitor to Mugshots' premises: his presence is known to the occupier (or its agents) and this presence is not objected to.

A limitation on the permission of visitors to enter some parts of the premises and not others can render the entrant a trespasser upon entry to the restricted area, provided proper steps have been taken to bring the limitation to the visitor's attention: *Gould* v *McAuliffe* (5). However, it is submitted that the shouting of a warning to 'come back' directed at a deaf child was insufficient to achieve any such limitation, and therefore Craig should be regarded as a visitor when he enters the room adjoining the waiting area.

Law of Tort – June 1998

Are Mugshots in breach of the 'common duty of care'?
Section 2(1) OLA 1957 imposes a common duty of care on occupiers in respect of all visitors to their premises. Section 2(2) states that the duty is:

> 'To take such care as in all the circumstances of the case is reasonable to see that the visitor will be reasonably safe in using the premises for the purposes for which he is invited or permitted by the occupier to be there.'

In deciding how much care Mugshots should reasonably have taken to ensure that Craig was reasonably safe on their premises, a number of factors will be taken into account, such as the nature of the danger, the steps necessary to remove it and the likelihood of injury resulting. In addition, s2(3)(a) OLA 1957 expressly provides that 'an occupier must be prepared for children to be less careful than adults.'

In order to exercise a reasonable degree of care in supervising Derek, it could be argued that Mugshots should have supervised Derek more carefully, ensuring that the shelving was properly secured whilst Derek was absent from the premises. Mugshots might also have closed off the work area by rendering the swing doors inoperable, assuming access to the room could have been avoided during normal business hours. It could be further argued that the oral warning was not enough to allow Craig to be reasonably safe (under s2(4)(a) OLA 1957), in that it failed to identify a specific danger in a specific place, and because Mugshots either knew, or ought to have realised (on the basis of what they had seen of Belinda and Craig) that Craig was deaf. It is possible that shouting a warning to a small boy is inadequate in any event.

Mugshots will undoubtedly attempt to argue that their warning (via their 'agent' employee, Ethel) was enough, in all the circumstances, to enable Craig to be reasonably safe (s2(4)(a) OLA 1957), and that their duty towards him was thereby discharged. In addition, Mugshots might argue that they were entitled to assume that a reasonable mother would not permit her very young child to be allowed to remain in the waiting area alone, especially if very deaf. At the very least, Belinda could have asked the receptionist to supervise her child, and in addition, warned her of Craig's deafness. Alternatively, Belinda might reasonably have been expected to satisfy herself that there were no immediate dangers facing Craig whilst she left him to have her photograph taken. In short, Mugshots would argue that they could not have foreseen that the unsecured shelving in the work area would be a danger to Craig, given Belinda's responsibility for her child's safety. On this point see *Phipps v Rochester Corporation* (6), a case in which the occupier of land was held not to have broken any duty of care in respect of a child of five years of age who was not accompanied by an adult.

If this last argument were to succeed, the view appears to be that Belinda herself would be liable as a joint tortfeasor to Craig in common law negligence. Mugshots would primarily be fully liable to Craig, but would have a right to recover a contribution from Belinda under the Civil Liability (Contribution) Act 1978: see Winfield and Jolowicz (7).

Have Mugshots discharged their duty to take reasonable care by adequate selection and supervision of an independent contractor under s2(4)(b) OLA 1957?
Mugshots will not be answerable to Craig under this provision if the following criteria are all satisfied.

1. There must have been 'faulty execution of any work of construction ... by an independent contractor employed by the occupier'. In practice, these words are given a broad and purposeful construction and it is submitted that they are wide enough to cover dangerously unguarded and unsecured work-in-progress, such as the shelving in the instant case.
2. Mugshots must have acted reasonably in entrusting the work to an independent contractor. It is submitted that it is most probably common commercial practice to engage an independent contractor to put up shelving, even if the job could probably have been undertaken by anyone in the firm with basic DIY skills. Thus, it is probably the case that Mugshots acted reasonably in hiring someone to carry out the work for them.
3. Mugshots must have taken reasonable care to ensure that Derek was competent to carry out the work. This will depend upon the reasons why Mugshots selected Derek to do the work in the first place, and whether they took steps to satisfy themselves that he had sufficient experience to do the job properly. It is clearly relevant to know whether Derek's job on the council involves work of a similar nature.
4. Mugshots must have taken reasonable care to check, if appropriate, that the 'work had been properly done'. Mugshots clearly failed to check that the shelving had been properly secured. Given that the work was not of a particularly technical nature, it is submitted that it would have been reasonable for them to have done so.

Thus it would appear from (4) above that Mugshots may remain answerable to Craig under OLA 1957, assuming that they are in breach of their common duty of care.

Liability in respect of Belinda's 'nervous shock'.
Assuming that Mugshots are liable to Craig under OLA 1957, or that Derek is liable as a non-occupier in negligence, Belinda may be able to claim as a secondary victim, ie one who was not personally involved in the accident nor placed in fear of suffering injury, but nonetheless perceived the consequences of a tort, suffering psychiatric illness as a result.

Two initial requirements which are immediately satisfied on the facts are as follows:

1. Belinda suffered a medically recognised psychiatric illness, ie severe depression: *Chadwick* v *British Transport Commission* (8); and
2. the illness resulted from a sudden shock.

There are a number of criteria which must be met if Belinda is to succeed in her claim. These criteria were first established by the House of Lords in *McLoughlin* v *O'Brian* (9) and subsequently refined in *Alcock* v *Chief Constable of South Yorkshire* (10). These criteria all seem to apply to Belinda, and can be summarised as follows.

1. It was reasonably foreseeable that Belinda would suffer psychiatric illness, as her relationship with the primary victim (Craig) was sufficiently close. In *McLoughlin* it was held that the relationship between parent and child was sufficiently proximate to recover.
2. Belinda's proximity to the accident or its 'immediate aftermath' was sufficiently close in both space and time. Belinda was in the same building as Craig when the accident occurred and she immediately ran to him when she heard his screams.

3. Belinda suffered psychiatric illness through hearing the accident and seeing its immediate aftermath.

It must be remembered that Belinda may be held partly responsible for Craig's accident and, if so, she may suffer a reduction in compensation on a finding that she was contributory negligent under the Law Reform (Contributory Negligence) Act 1945.

References

(1)   [1966] AC 552
(2)   [1968] 1 WLR 1028
(3)   [1984] 134 NLJ 723
(4)   [1981] 3 All ER 405
(5)   [1941] 2 All ER 527
(6)   [1955] 1 QB 450
(7)   Winfield and Jolowicz, *Tort* (15th edn, 1998) at p301
(8)   [1967] 2 All ER 945
(9)   [1983] 1 AC 410
(10) [1992] 1 AC 310

Question Five

'Causation in tort should be a matter of common sense and not of philosophical theory.'
Discuss.

Suggested Solution

General Comment

It is unlikely that candidates will have had a detailed knowledge of any of the philosophical approaches to the issue of causation, and so what was required here was comment on the extent to which the rules could be said to reflect a commonsense approach to the imposition of liability. The focus was primarily on causation in fact. However, it would have been reasonable to include discussion on intervening cause, or even remoteness of damage.

Skeleton Solution

Introduce by explaining briefly the function of the rules of causation in tort – causation in fact – explain and illustrate 'but-for' test – explain how the rule runs into difficulty in cases involving multiple and successive causes and how the courts have modified their approach to achieve a result which accords with common sense – causation in law – rules on intervening act – based on common sense?

Suggested Solution

One way in which the law reflects notions of individual responsibility is by ensuring that a link exists between the conduct of a defendant (an act or an omission) and some harmful consequence before liability can be imposed. It is this link which justifies fixing the defendant with liability and requiring him to pay compensation. The nature of the link has been the subject of some philosophical debate and a number of possible approaches have been identified. However, the law has required the adoption of a small number of practical commonsense approaches which can be readily understood and applied to a range of real life factual scenarios. It is these approaches, and the extent to which they accord with common sense, which is discussed below.

The question of causation in tort can be approached in two stages. The first involves asking whether, as a matter of fact, the defendant's negligence was a cause of the claimant's loss. It is this so-called 'causation in fact' test which has received the most attention from philosophers. The second stage involves a consideration of whether, as a matter of law, the defendant ought to be held liable for the damage which he has in fact caused. Winfield and

Jolowicz (1) point out that this second stage involves the consideration of issues of fairness and legal policy.

Causation in fact

This stage merely establishes a factual link between the defendant's act or omission and the claimant's loss. The test normally adopted is the so-called 'but-for' test. In *Cork v Kirby MacLean Ltd* (2) Lord Denning stated:

> 'If the damage would not have happened but for a particular fault, then the fault is the cause of the damage; if it would have happened just the same, fault or no fault, the fault is not the cause of the damage.'

The case usually quoted to illustrate this point is *Barnett v Chelsea and Kensington Hospital Management Committee* (3) in which the death of the plaintiff's husband was held not to have been caused by an employee doctor's refusal to examine and failure to diagnose arsenical poisoning. It was found that it would have been too late to have saved the deceased by the time he arrival at hospital in any event.

Whilst the 'but-for' test certainly represents a commonsense approach to establishing a factual link between claimant and defendant, it is nothing more than a preliminary test to eliminate truly irrelevant causes, and is almost always satisfied in practice. However, the test breaks down in cases where there is more than one cause of the harmful consequence, its application leading to a result which defies common sense. An example given by Professor Atiyah illustrates the point nicely (4). Two fires started independently by A and B unite and spread to C's house which is destroyed. In applying the test 'but for A's negligence would C have suffered loss?' the answer would be yes, given that B's negligence would have caused the same loss in any event. The question would be resolved the same way in respect of B's negligence and thus neither party would be held liable for C's loss. However, the courts would almost certainly adopt a modified, commonsense approach in order to fix such defendants with liability. As Lord Wright said in *Yorkshire Dale Steamship Co Ltd v Minister of War Transport* (5) 'causation is to be understood as the man in the street, and not as either the scientist or the metaphysician, would understand it.'

The approach of the courts has been to resolve cases involving multiple possible causes according to notions of the burden of proof. An initial case of difficulty was the House of Lord's decision in *McGhee v National Coal Board* (6) in which an employee was allowed to recover compensation against his employer in negligence after having contracted dermatitis, possibly through the lack of proper washing facilities at his place of work. Although the medical evidence was insufficient to establish that the skin disease had been caused by prolonged exposure to sweat and grime, recovery was still possible as the defendant's breach of duty was said to have materially increased the risk of the employee contracting the disease. It seems that this 'robust and pragmatic' approach was influenced more by considerations of policy than logic, Lord Wilberforce pointing out that (given the evidential difficulties for the claimant in establishing causation in such cases):

> 'It is the creator of the risk who, ex hypothesi, must be taken to have foreseen the possibility of damage, who should bear its consequences.'

However, the current approach of the courts in cases of multiple possible cause is to require that the claimant prove the defendant's negligence was a probable cause, ie a more likely cause than the possible alternatives. Thus in *Hotson* v *East Berkshire Area Health Authority* (7) the House of Lords disallowed a claim for serious disabilities arising after an accident in which a boy injured his hip joint. On the facts, there was a 25 per cent chance that the defendant's failure to promptly diagnose the condition resulted in permanent disability (and a 75 per cent chance that the condition would have developed anyway, even if the plaintiff had been properly treated) and so the plaintiff failed to prove his case. Similarly in *Wilsher* v *Essex Area Health Authority* (8), conflicting medical evidence was such that the trial judge had failed to identify whether retinal damage sustained by a patient during birth was caused by the negligent administration of an excess of oxygen by the doctor, or by a number of alternative possible non-negligent causes. The case was sent for retrial on the causation issue, the claimant being required to prove his case on the balance of probabilities. Thus, it could be said that one commonsense approach adopted in *McGhee*, allowing a claimant to recover damages in the face of the evidential difficulties in proving causation, has given way to another commonsense approach which insists that all cases must be proved on the balance of probabilities, thereby creating consistency and certainty in the law.

Another problem with the 'but-for' test occurs where the claimant's injuries are attributable to successive causes, only the first of which is related to the defendant's negligence. In *Baker* v *Willoughby* (9) the plaintiff suffered injury to his leg as a result of the defendant's negligence, resulting in ongoing pain and discomfort and a loss of earning capacity. The plaintiff took up a new job after the accident, but was shot in the same leg by armed robbers whilst at work, necessitating an amputation. The defendant argued that his liability should be limited to the loss suffered by the plaintiff before the date of the robbery. The argument was rejected by the House of Lords, because even if the robbers could be sued for damages, they would have taken their victim as they had found him and would only have had to compensate the plaintiff for the loss of a bad leg. This would be manifestly unjust as the plaintiff would have been left uncompensated following the robbery for the difference between a good and a bad leg. The House in *Baker* therefore adopted a commonsense approach in order to do justice to the claimant.

However, *Baker* was subsequently thrown into doubt by the decision of the House of Lords in *Jobling* v *Associated Dairies Ltd* (10). The defendant's liability to pay compensation in respect of the back injury sustained by the plaintiff at work (arising through a breach of statutory duty) was cut short by the independent onset, before trial, of a naturally occurring back condition. This condition was such that it would, in itself, have rendered the plaintiff unable to work. The Lords in *Jobling* were critical of the decision in *Baker*. It was noted that damages are generally reduced to take account of the 'vicissitudes of life', ie the possibility that the plaintiff's working life might be cut short by future events such as early death or unemployment. Where such an event took place before trial, the defendant should not be forced to continue to pay damages for future loss of earnings, as to do so would be to place the claimant in a better position than he would otherwise have been in had the tort not been committed.

There is clearly a conflict between the decisions of *Baker* and *Jobling*, although it has been suggested that *Baker* will continue to apply in cases involving two successive tortious causes. The decision in *Baker* was driven by a commonsense approach which aimed to prevent the plaintiff from being under-compensated. The decision in *Jobling* was driven by an equally logical desire to prevent the plaintiff from being overcompensated. It is therefore submitted that the courts will adopt a pragmatic, case-by-case analysis of causation rather than applying a uniform philosophical approach, in order to reach decisions which may be regarded as a matter of common sense. However, as we have seen, the commonsense approach of one judge can differ from another, and it should not be supposed that consistency will be found in the authorities. As Lord Sumner pointed out in *Weld-Blundell* v *Stephens* (11):

> 'The trial of an action for damages is not a scientific inquest into a mixed sequence of phenomena, or an historical investigation of the chapter of events ... It is a practical enquiry.'

One final area worthy of mention relates to the second stage of enquiry, ie whether, as a matter of law, the defendant ought to be held responsible for the damage which he has, in fact, caused. The starting point here might be to consider the rules relating to remoteness of damage. However, for the purposes of this essay it is more instructive to consider those situations in which the damage suffered by the claimant cannot be recovered, even though the 'but-for' test is established, because the courts consider that an intervening act has broken the link between the defendant's negligence and the claimant's loss. It is submitted that these novus actus interveniens scenarios are all firmly based upon common sense, and a desire to do justice on the individual facts of each case.

The first category is where, following the negligence of the defendant, some unreasonable act of the claimant (going beyond mere contributory negligence) renders the injury suffered too remote from the original act or omission. In *McKew* v *Holland & Hannen & Cubitts (Scotland) Ltd* (12) the plaintiff, having suffered mild injury to his leg as a result of the negligence of the defendants, suffered further injury when his leg gave away on a steep flight of stairs. It was held that the plaintiff was unable to recover further compensation, as his unreasonable act of descending the steep stairs with no handrail broke the chain of causation.

An intervening act of nature which is independent of the negligence of the defendant may also serve to break the chain of causation. Such was the case in *Carslogie Steamship Co* v *Royal Norwegian Government* (13). Here the plaintiff's ship suffered extensive damage in a storm on a journey it would not otherwise have made, but for a delay caused by the defendant's negligence. The storm was treated as a supervening event, breaking the chain of causation and relieving the defendant of liability for the subsequent storm damage.

Finally, the unreasonable intervening act of a third party may break the chain of causation where it takes the form of a negligent or reckless independent cause. Thus, in *Knightley* v *Johns* (14), a negligent defendant who caused an accident, blocking a tunnel, was not held liable for injuries sustained by a police motorcyclist who was negligently instructed by the officer in charge to drive back into the tunnel against the flow of traffic.

The courts have much more discretion to exercise their common sense in these cases, by allocating blame between the two defendants whose negligence contributed towards the claimant's loss. Thus in *Rouse* v *Squires* (15), a negligent driver jack-knifed his lorry across the road, causing an accident. Several minutes later, the second defendant negligently collided with the vehicles involved in the first accident, causing the plaintiff's death. It was held that both defendants' actions were operative causes of the accident and liability was allocated to the first defendant in the proportion of 25 per cent.

References

(1)   Winfield and Jolowicz, *Tort* (15th edn, 1998) at p196
(2)   [1952] 2 All ER 402
(3)   [1969] 1 QB 428
(4)   Cane, Peter (ed), *Atiyah's Accidents, Compensation and the Law* (4th edn, 1987)
(5)   [1942] AC 691
(6)   [1973] 1 WLR 1
(7)   [1987] AC 50
(8)   [1988] 1 All ER 871
(9)   [1970] AC 467
(10) [1982] AC 794
(11) [1920] AC 956
(12) [1969] 3 All ER 1621
(13) [1952] AC 292
(14) [1982] 1 WLR 349
(15) [1973] QB 889

Question Six

Richard worked as a gardener with the Peony District Council. He was planting out a bed of rose bushes which the council had purchased from the Floribunda Nurseries. The bushes had been treated with a spray to repel greenfly. It is known that a number of people react to the spray for some days after it has been applied. Richard began to feel breathless, but, before anyone could come to his assistance, he had collapsed. It appears that he is abnormally allergic to the spray. He has suffered permanent brain damage. He is happy and in no physical pain but is unable to look after himself, to work or to pursue his hobby of darts. His mother Stella has given up her job in a supermarket to look after him, but she is quite elderly and it is expected that Richard will eventually have to go into a home.

Advise Richard (a) as to any claims he may have in tort and (b) as to the assessment of damages.

Suggested Solution

General Comment

It was important that candidates noted the ambiguity in the facts of this question. It was not made clear whether it was the council or the nursery who were responsible for the spraying of the rosebushes, and the precise nature of liability would have varied accordingly. Candidates could have chosen to deal with employers' liability first, although it might have been more logical initially to consider Floribunda's liability for the possible supply of a defective product. This is because an employer's vicarious liability for the provision of defective equipment depends upon the fault of the third party who supplied it.

Skeleton Solution

Product liability – examine Floribunda's potential liability under the Consumer Protection Act 1987 – is a rosebush a 'product' within the meaning of the Act? – discuss the possibility of liability at common law under the narrow rule in *Donoghue* v *Stevenson* – employers' liability – is Peony vicariously liable for providing Richard with defective equipment under the Employers' Liability (Defective Equipment) Act 1969? – is a rosebush 'equipment' within the meaning of the Act? – if Peony was responsible for the spraying of the rosebush, are they in breach of their non-delegable duty to provide a safe system of working? – the assessment of damages – identify the aim of damages in tort and explain the heads of loss relevant to Richard's circumstances, under which damages will be awarded – make particular reference to future loss of earnings, the provision of care by a relative and loss of amenity.

Law of Tort – June 1998

Suggested Solution

a) *Claims in tort: liability for defective products – Floribunda Nurseries*

If, as seems likely, Florinbunda were themselves responsible for growing the rose bushes and for spraying them with the greenfly repellent, the question arises as to Floribunda's liability as producers of a defective product. Section 2(1) Consumer Protection Act 1987 provides that 'where any damage is caused wholly or partly by a defect in a product, every person to whom subsection (2) … applies shall be liable for the damage.' Section 2(2) lists a number of potential defendants, including the producer of the product, further defined in s1(2)(c) as including a person who carried out (for example in relation to agricultural products) an industrial or other process.

An immediate problem for Richard here is that agricultural products, defined in s1(2) as including 'any produce of the soil' are excluded from the provisions of the Act unless they have undergone an 'industrial process' before supply. The definition is aimed at the processing of raw foodstuffs so that, for example, the processing of meet into beef burgers would be caught by the provisions of the Act. It is submitted that the mere spraying of agricultural produce would not be regarded as an industrial process, and so the rosebushes are not 'products' for the purposes of the Act. If the spraying of crops were to be regarded as an industrial process, the exemption of agricultural produce from the provisions of the Act would be meaningless and ineffective.

Common law

The so-called narrow rule laid down by Lord Atkin in *Donoghue v Stevenson* (1) imposes a duty on manufacturers of products to the ultimate consumer in certain circumstances:

> '… a manufacturer of products, which he sells in such a form as to show that he intends them to reach the ultimate consumer in the form in which they left him, with no reasonable possibility of intermediate examination, and with the knowledge that the absence of reasonable care in the preparation or putting up of the products will result in an injury to the consumer's life or property, owes a duty to the consumer to take that reasonable care.'

The duty as originally defined has been extended in many respects, and could apply to Richard's circumstances for the following reasons.

1. Whilst the grower of plants might not be regarded as a 'manufacturer' in the traditional sense, the duty has been extended to cover a range of persons who create dangers in relation to products, such as repairers, erectors and builders. It is submitted that growers would also fall within the scope of the duty.
2. The duty, whilst originally relating to food and drink, has been held to apply to a range of products, eg tombstones and cars, so rosebushes are presumably covered.
3. The duty extends to the ultimate user of the product as well as those within close proximity of it. It is submitted that Richard, as a gardener who plants the product, is within sufficiently close proximity to come within the scope of the duty.
4. The possibility of an 'intermediate examination' of the rosebushes by Richard is unlikely to exonerate the nursery. The presence of a chemical residue on a plant could not be discovered by a reasonable examination, unless a specific warning had been provided: *Andrews v Hopkinson* (2).

5. It will be for Richard to prove that the nursery failed to take reasonable care by spraying the rosebushes with a dangerous insect repellent. This should not cause any great difficulty. If it can be shown that the Council were not responsible for the spraying, then on the balance of probabilities, it must have been Floribunda who did so. In view of the known risks associated with this particular insect repellent, a finding of breach of duty appears likely.
6. Richard's abnormal sensitivity to the spray does not render the serious physical injuries he sustained too remote from any negligence on the part of Floribunda. A tortfeasor takes his victim as he finds him. So long as physical injury was foreseeable (there were known risks of adverse reactions to this chemical spray lasting some days after application) the claimant can recover damages, even if the extent of those injuries could not have been foreseen: *Smith v Leech, Brain & Co* (3).

It would appear that Richard's claim in respect of a defective product would therefore lie in common law negligence, rather than under the Consumer Protection Act 1987, due to the exclusion of agricultural products from the scope of the latter.

Liability of Peony District Council as employers

Peony District Council's liability to Richard as his employer will depend upon who was responsible for the application of the insect repellent. If the nursery were responsible for the spraying, then Peony may be vicariously liable for the supply of defective 'equipment' attributable to the fault of a third party under s1(1) Employers' Liability (Defective Equipment) Act 1969. If the spray was applied by the Council, then it would be more appropriate to consider whether Peony were in breach of their non-delegable common law duty to provide a safe system of work.

Employers' Liability (Defective Equipment) Act 1969

Section 1(1) states that:

> 'Where ...
> (a) an employee suffers personal injury in the course of his employment in consequence of a defect in equipment provided by his employer for the purposes of his employer's business; and
> (b) the defect is attributable wholly or partly to the fault of a third party (whether identified or not),
> the injury shall be deemed to be also attributable to negligence on the part of the employer.'

In other words, the Council will be vicariously liable for defective equipment supplied to Richard for the purposes of his job, if the defect arose through the fault of Floribunda Nurseries.

The main issue here is whether a rosebush could be said to be 'equipment' within the meaning of the Act. Section 1(3) defines 'equipment' as 'any plant and machinery, vehicle, aircraft and clothing.' In fact, the courts have adopted a wide, purposive approach to the interpretation of this section. For example, in *Knowles v Liverpool City Council* (4) the House of Lords held that a flagstone, which broke whilst being handled by an employee, causing personal injury, should be regarded as equipment even though it was, in fact, 'material upon which the employee used the equipment.' Thus it is clearly arguable that a rosebush, which will have been planted with the use of gardening tools, should be regarded as 'equipment' within the meaning of the Act. If Richard can show that the spray residue caused his injury and that there must, on the balance of probabilities, have been negligence on the part of Floribunda Nurseries (see above), then the Council as well as Floribunda will be liable to him, even though the Council were not to blame.

Safe system of work
If Peony District Council was responsible for the application of the greenfly repellent, then there is likely to have been a breach of their duty as employers to take reasonable care in devising and operating a safe system of work. Such a breach of duty would arise from the use of a known allergen to spray the bushes rather than some safer alternative, and the failure to provide adequate warnings, instructions and personal protective equipment to those employees handling the plants which have been sprayed with the substance. As explained above, Richard's abnormal sensitivity to the spray residue will not render the serious physical injuries he sustained too remote from any negligence on the part of his employer.

b) *The assessment of damages*
Any award of damages will be payable as a lump sum, unless the parties were to agree to a structured settlement. The aim of such an award will be to restore Richard, in so far as money will allow, to the position he was in before the tort(s) took place. An award of damages is usually considered in two parts: 'special damages' covering precisely calculable losses, normally arising pre-trial, and 'general damages', which are not capable of precise mathematical calculation and normally arise post-trial. It is also customary to classify losses sustained as being either pecuniary or non-pecuniary in nature.

Pecuniary losses: loss of earnings
This will include any loss of Richard's earnings both before and after trial. The large part of the award will be for loss of salary post-trial, as Richard is now unemployable on a long-term basis. Any award will include prospective earnings during any 'lost years' due to a reduced life expectancy and loss of pension rights associated with a future loss of salary.

The court will award Richard a lump sum which, when invested, will be sufficient to produce an income equal to the loss of his future salary. The calculation is approached in two stages. The court will first assess Richard's net annual loss, by taking his gross earnings at the date of the accident, but also making an allowance for the possibility of an increase in pay or for promotion. Once this sum has been calculated, a deduction will be made for the income tax and social security contributions he would have paid on his earnings.

The court will then select a multiplier based upon the likely duration of the disability. However, this will not be the same as the number of years Richard would have worked before retirement, because the courts apply a reduction to take account of the possibility that future events might have cut his working life short, eg early death or unemployment. A reduction is also applied to take account of the fact that a lump sum payment will produce an investment income of its own.

Medical expenses reasonably incurred
This includes the cost of nursing care and travel expenses to and from hospital. The cost of nursing care provided by Stella can be recovered by Richard himself: *Hunt v Severs* (5). In *Housecroft v Burnett* (6) it was decided that where a relative gives up work to look after the claimant, the court will award reasonable recompense to the carer, but the ceiling on such an award is the commercial rate for providing such care. It is unlikely that Stella would be paid more than her existing salary whilst she is still able to look after Richard, if her current salary is less than the commercial rate of remuneration for professional nursing care. However, a full commercial rate ought to be recoverable for the years during which Richard will have to spend in a home. The damages awarded in respect of the carer will be held on trust for Stella by Richard: *Cunningham v Harrison* (7). Further deductions will be made to reflect any social security benefits that Richard has received as a result of his injuries since the accident.

Non-pecuniary losses
Richard's non-pecuniary losses include his loss of amenity, ie the loss of capacity to engage in activities which he enjoyed before trial (playing darts) and compensation for his actual injuries. The amounts awarded under these heads are usually assessed by reference to past cases. An award would usually be made for any pain and suffering endured by the claimant; however, Richard appears to be perfectly happy and in no pain, and so damages are unlikely to be awarded under this head.

Finally, Richard will receive interest on the lump sum payment reflecting the lapse in time between the accident and the trial.

References

(1) [1932] AC 562
(2) [1957] 1 QB 229
(3) [1962] 2 QB 405
(4) [1993] 4 All ER 321
(5) [1994] 2 All ER 385
(6) [1986] 1 All ER 332
(7) [1973] QB 942

Question Seven

Chill and Douche, two members of the building inspections team in the Loamshire Fire Brigade, carried out an inspection of the engineering building at Loamshire University. They reported that the notice boards were a fire hazard and that, if notices continued to be displayed anywhere in the corridors and staircases other than in specially constructed glass cases, they would seek a court order closing the building. At a meeting with student representatives a few days later, Flame, the Dean of Engineering, remarked that because of 'the Hitlerite tendency' of the local fire brigade, he had to prohibit students from displaying any notices advertising their societies. The next issue of the Student Union newspaper carried a banner headline reading, ' "FIRE INSPECTORS ARE FASCIST SCUM", SAYS DEAN.' Copies of this newspaper are handed out to students on the campus, and are also prominently on sale in local newsagents.

Advise the parties as to any possible claims in defamation.

Suggested Solution

General Comment

This ought to have been a relatively straightforward question for candidates who had a sufficient understanding of the principles of defamation and were aware of the changes brought about by the Defamation Act 1996. It was necessary for candidates to clearly organise their answers, by dealing with the separate potential actions disclosed by the facts under different headings.

Skeleton Solution

Action by Chill and Douche against Flame in slander – was this slander actionable per se? – were the words defamatory? – could Chill and Douche claim as individuals in respect of a 'group' slander? – were there any defences available to Flame, eg qualified privilege and fair comment? – action by Chill and Douche against the newspaper and others in libel – were the words defamatory? – could Chill and Douche claim as individuals in respect of a 'group' libel? – defences available, eg offer to make amends? – action by Flame against the newspaper and others in libel – defences available, eg fair comment and offer to make amends.

Suggested Solution

The question involves a number of potential claims in the tort of defamation, arising from untrue statements which have injured the reputation of those concerned.

Action by Chill and Douche against Flame in slander
Spoken statements are not in a permanent form and are therefore classified as slanders. Generally, slanders are only actionable if the claimants can show that they have suffered special damage, ie have suffered a loss which is capable of being estimated in money. However, there are a number of exceptional cases where slanders become actionable per se, such as where the statement imputes unfitness to one's trade or calling.

Flame's description of the 'Hitlerite tendency' of the local fire brigade was clearly calculated to disparage Chill and Douche in their profession or calling, and therefore no proof of special damage will be required on their part: s2 Defamation Act 1952.

There is no single definition of a defamatory statement; however, they have been held to include 'words which tend to lower the plaintiff in the estimation of right-thinking members of society generally' (*Sim* v *Stretch* (1)), possibly exposing him to 'hatred, contempt or ridicule' (*Parmiter* v *Coupland and Another* (2)), or causing people to shun him or lose confidence in him: *Youssoupoff* v *Metro-Goldwyn-Mayer* (3). Words may be defamatory 'even though they neither impute disgraceful conduct to the plaintiff nor any lack of skill or efficiency in the conduct of his trade or business or professional activity, if they hold him up to contempt, scorn or ridicule, or tend to exclude him from society': *Berkoff* v *Burchill* (4). It is submitted that the suggestion that the local fire brigade display 'Hitlerite tendencies' is likely to induce hatred, ridicule and contempt to those at the meeting and even impute disgraceful conduct on the part of the inspectors. On the other hand, Flame might argue that, if the words were uttered in a fit of temper, they should have been understood as amounting to nothing more than vulgar abuse, and therefore not defamatory: *Fields* v *Davis* (5).

However, a more fundamental issue here is whether Chill and Douche can claim that they have been defamed as individuals when the comments made related to the local fire brigade as a whole. Generally, where the defamatory statement has been directed at a group or class of persons, no individual belonging to that class may sue, unless there is something in the words or the circumstances in which they were uttered which might identify the claimant in particular: *Knupffer* v *London Express Newspapers Limited* (6). Alternatively, if the group which is alleged to have been defamed is very limited in size, then the statement might be understood as referring to the claimant: *Browne* v *D C Thompson* (7).

It is submitted that Chill and Douche are likely to experience problems establishing that they, as individuals, have been slandered. Flame's comments were directed at the local fire brigade and made to a group of student representatives several days after the inspection took place. If anyone present at the meeting was to have observed Chill and Douche at work in the building, then Flame's comments might have been taken as being directed at them individually. Otherwise, it is likely that the local fire brigade consists of too many individuals for the comments to be taken as referring to any one of them. However, it should be noted that the subsequent repetition of Flame's words indicate that they were understood as referring specifically to fire inspectors.

Defences: qualified privilege
The effect of this defence is to protect the maker of the statement from liability in defamation provided he acted honestly and without malice. It will be for the claimants, Chill and Douche, to prove that Flame was actuated by malice, ie that he had no honest belief in

the truth of his statement, or that he used the occasion for a purpose extending beyond that for which the qualified privilege existed: *Horrocks v Lowe* (8).

However, only statements made in certain circumstance enjoy a qualified privilege. One set of circumstances is 'where the person who makes a communication has an interest, or a duty, legal, social or moral, to make it to the person to whom it is made, and the person to whom it is made has a corresponding interest or duty to receive it. This reciprocity is essential': *Adam v Ward* (9) per Lord Atkinson.

It is clear that Flame has a legal duty (under Health and Safety legislation) or at the very least a social/moral duty to instruct the students not to display notices given the apparent hazards involved and the possible closure of the building. To this extent the students have an interest in receiving the information. However, Flame's comments regarding 'Hitlerite tendencies' indicate that he has used the occasion for a purpose extending beyond that for which the qualified privilege exists, ie to disparage the inspectors. It is submitted that the claimants could rebut a provisional finding of qualified privilege and prove that Flame was actuated by malice.

Fair comment
This defence is relevant where comment is honestly made on a matter of public interest. The defendant must prove four elements.

1. The comments related to a matter of public interest 'such as to effect people at large, so that they may be legitimately interested in, or concerned at, what is going on; or what may happen to them or others': *London Artists Ltd v Littler* (10) per Lord Denning. The prohibition of the display of notices affects the students of the faculty and their ability to continue to use the building, and so Flame's comments are clearly in the public interest.
2. The statement was one of opinion, not fact. It is submitted that Flame's comments regarding the inspectors' 'Hitlerite tendencies' were clearly opinion, based upon his experience of their previous conduct.
3. The comments were fair in all the circumstances of the case. This is an objective test based upon whether any fair-minded person could honestly express the opinion in question, even if it was exaggerated, obstinate or prejudiced. It is difficult to apply this test conclusively to the facts. It might be thought that the inspectors had been overzealous in discharging their duties and that Flame had a reasonable basis for his comments, even if he over-exaggerated. On the other hand, it might be thought that Flame's words were so overstated that his motives must have been improper, and consequently his comments would be regarded as unfair.
4. The comments were not inspired by malice, ie spite, ill-will or any other improper motive.

Is Flame liable for the republication of his defamatory words?
A maker of a defamatory statement may also find himself liable for the damage caused by the repetition of the defamatory statement by a third party, at least where that repetition was reasonably foreseeable. An unauthorised repetition of such a statement by an independent third party (here the Student Union Newspaper and the various distributors) may well be regarded as a novus actus interveniens breaking the chain of causation, provided Flame

could not reasonably have anticipated the repetition of his slander as a natural and probable consequence of his original comments: *Slipper v British Broadcasting Corporation* (11).

Claim by Chill and Douche against the Student Union Newspaper and others for libel
Every time a defamatory statement is repeated, the tort is committed again and a fresh cause of action arises. Anyone who participated in the publication of the Student Union Newspaper or its mechanical distribution is potentially liable, subject to a range of defences. Such persons would include the author of the headline, the editor, the printer, the proprietor of the newspaper, the distributors (on campus) and the newsagents.

The headline is potentially a libel as it exists in a permanent form. The words used in the headline are stronger than those originally uttered by Flame and possibly more defamatory. The newspaper might argue that the headline merely reported vulgar abuse spoken by the Dean, and should not be understood to be defamatory of the inspectors themselves. They would argue that an ordinary hypothetical reader, who was not 'avid for scandal', would not necessary believe in the truth of the statement, simply in the fact that it was said. On the other hand it could be argued that an ordinary reader who is neither 'naïve' nor 'unduly suspicious' might read into it an implication of disgraceful conduct on the part of the inspectors 'more readily than a lawyer' having 'indulged in a certain amount of loose thinking': *Hartt v Newspaper Publishing plc* (12). Ultimately, whether the words uttered are reasonably capable of being defamatory is a question of law for the judge before the matter can be put to the jury.

The same problems arise here as to whether Chill and Douche could be said to have been defamed as individuals, given that the statement was aimed at a group of persons. The headline is more specific in that it refers to fire inspectors rather than members of the local fire brigade. Assuming the article goes on to explain the background to the Dean's comments, it is possible that the headline could be taken as inferentially referring to Chill and Douche by those with special local knowledge of the inspectorate: *Morgan v Odhams Press Limited* (13).

Defences: offer to make amends
Under s2(4) Defamation Act 1996 it is open to the newspaper to make an offer to make amends by publishing a suitable correction and apology and to pay compensation. If Chill and Douche were to accept such an offer, any proceedings against the paper would be brought to an end, and if the parties were not able to agree on compensation, this amount would be decided by the court. Under s4, if an offer is not accepted, the fact that the offer has been made is a defence to defamation proceedings unless the claimants can prove that the statement referred to them and was both false and defamatory.

A defence of fair comment would be bound to fail in this case, because the introduction of the word 'scum' seems to indicate an improper motive or malice on the part of the author, thus rendering the comment unfair.

Action by Flame against the Student Union Newspaper and others in libel
The essence of such a claim would be that the newspaper exaggerated Flame's comments in a way that affects his professional standing and raises a question as to whether he is discharging his duties in an appropriate manner. The imputation of 'disgraceful conduct' on Flame's part may hold him up to contempt, scorn or ridicule and lower him in the

estimation of right-thinking people. The headline refers to Flame personally and so the only question remaining is whether the newspaper can avail itself of a defence.

Defence: fair comment
If this article is simply about the Dean's outburst, then it might be said to be of public interest in that it calls into question Flame's professional conduct and whether he is discharging his duties in an appropriate manner. A bare statement of fact (for example a verbatim report of Flame's comments) cannot found the defence. However, the words 'fascist scum' seem to represent an opinion of the true meaning of Flame's original words.

It would have to be decided whether a fair-minded person could honestly express the opinion that the Dean, in his original comments, had really been suggesting that the inspectors were 'fascist scum'. The addition of the word 'scum' and the fact that the statement is portrayed as a direct quote (which is clearly inaccurate) might indicate some improper motive to portray the Dean in a bad light, and as such the defence would fail. An offer to make amends to the Dean could also apply here.

References

(1) [1936] 2 All ER 1237
(2) [1840] 6 M & W 105
(3) (1934) 50 TLR 581
(4) [1996] 4 All ER 1008
(5) [1955] CLY 1543
(6) [1944] AC 116
(7) 1912 SC 359
(8) [1975] AC 135
(9) [1917] AC 309
(10) [1969] 2 QB 375
(11) [1991] 1 QB 283
(12) (1989) The Times 7 November
(13) [1971] 1 WLR 1239

Question Eight

a) Discuss the concept of necessity as a defence to an action in trespasss.
b) Hilda enters hospital for major abdominal surgery. Ingrid, the surgical registrar, describes the nature of the operation to her and she signs a form consenting to the surgery. During the operation Ingrid notices that Hilda's appendix is diseased and is likely to cause her serious problems in a year or two. She therefore removes it. Hilda is annoyed when she discovers that this has happened.
   Advise her.

Suggested Solution

General Comment

Candidates would have needed a very detailed knowledge of the defences to actions in trespass, particularly in respect of trespasses to the person, in order to do justice to this question. It is therefore unsurprising that few candidates chose to answer this question in the exam.

Skeleton Solution

a) Discuss the limited nature of the defence of necessity to actions in both trespass to property and to the person, using past cases by way of illustration.
b) Discuss whether the removal of Hilda's appendix might have been covered by the terms of her original written consent – if Hilda's consent was not expressly provided, might the courts imply such consent? – finally, discuss whether the defence of necessity might justify additional procedures being carried out where other medical conditions are discovered during an operation.

Suggested Solution

a) Necessity is, by definition, an extremely limited defence in trespass as it allows a defendant to lawfully protect his, or another's, person or property, even though the result is that an innocent person suffers a loss in the process. It is likely that the defence will only be available in emergency situations where it is necessary for private citizens to avert immediate and serious dangers to life or property, and where the citizen acts reasonably in all the circumstances. Thus, defendants who take personal action, when a call to the emergency services would have been a reasonable alternative course of action, are unlikely to avail themselves of the defence.
   On this basis, campaigners against field trials of genetically modified plants had no

defence to an action in trespass after entering land to destroy some of the crops, even though they claimed such action was necessary to raise public awareness and to protect the public: *Monsanto plc v Tilly* (1). In *Southwark London Borough Council v Williams* (2) necessity was also held to be no defence to actions in trespass brought against homeless persons squatting in empty local authority housing, Lord Denning stating that otherwise, necessity '… would be an excuse for all sorts of wrongdoing. So the courts must, for the sake of law and order, take a firm stand.'

However, necessity has been successfully used as a defence to trespass to property in a variety of circumstances such as the following.

1. The prevention, by diversion, of flood water from entering a defendant's land, with the result that a neighbour's land was flooded: *Home Brewery plc v William Davis & Co (Loughborough) Ltd* (3).
2. The prevention of a plague of locusts from entering the defendant's land (achieved by entering the land of a third party) with the result that the insects re-entered the plaintiff's land, destroying crops: *Greyvensteyn v Hattingh* (4).
3. The firing, by a police officer, of a CS gas cylinder into a building in order to flush out a dangerous psychopath: *Rigby v Chief Constable of Northamptonshire* (5). However, whilst the defence was held to apply in the circumstances, damages were awarded against the defendant as the officer responsible was found to have been negligent in firing the cylinder without having fire fighting equipment to hand.
4. The throwing of goods overboard in a storm in order to save the passengers on a ship: *Mouse's Case* (6).

Necessity is also a limited defence to trespasses against the person. Most cases have arisen where medical treatment has been administered without a patient's consent, but even here the courts have taken an extremely restrictive approach to the availability of the defence, the sanctity of the human body being a fundamental basic principle.

Necessity would be applicable in those circumstances where a doctor is forced to give medical treatment to an unconscious patient in order to preserve life or prevent permanent damage to health. It might also extend to the administration of treatment to a conscious adult who is temporarily or permanently incompetent to give consent by reason of mental illness or because of the undue influence of others. For example, in *F v West Berkshire Area Health Authority* (7) the House of Lords allowed the defence of necessity to justify the sterilisation of a 36-year-old woman who was a voluntary patient in a mental hospital. It was held that the defence would be available in similar circumstances where a reasonable body of medical opinion was in favour of allowing the treatment in the best interests of the patient. Not only would treatment be justified in order to save life or to prevent permanent injury, but also in cases of routine medical treatment.

However, the defence will not operate where a mentally competent patient refuses life-saving treatment provided there is a full understanding of the consequences of that decision. This principle extends to the refusal of a caesarean section, even if that would mean the death of the mother's unborn child: *Re M B (Caesarean Section)* (8). Nor could the defence be used to justify the force-feeding of prisoners on hunger strike: *Secretary of State for the Home Department v Robb* (9).

b) The issues to be decided here are whether Hilda has in fact given her consent (express or implied) to the removal of her appendix and if not, whether its removal by the hospital was justified on the grounds of necessity. The basic position was stated by Lord Brandon in *F v West Berkshire Area Health Authority*:

> 'At common law, a doctor cannot lawfully operate on adult patients of sound mind ... without their consent. If a doctor were to operate on such patients, or give them other treatment, without their consent, he would commit the actionable tort of trespass to the person.'

In other words, the hospital may have committed a battery on Hilda in going beyond the scope of the original abdominal surgery. Whether such a battery has taken place here will depend upon the scope of the defences available to the hospital.

Did Hilda provide her express consent to the removal of her appendix?
We are told that Hilda signed a consent form covering, at the very least, major abdominal surgery. Such written consents normally contain a declaration, on the part of the patient, that the nature and effect of the treatment has been explained to them, and provided that the patient has in fact been advised of the broad nature of the operation by a doctor, consent will have been lawfully given. Whether Hilda has expressly consented to the removal of her appendix appears, therefore, to depend upon how closely this further procedure matched the precise nature of the operation previously explained to her. It is possible that the diseased appendix related to the condition originally requiring surgery, in which case Hilda's actual consent is more likely to authorise the removal of the organ. Another possibility is that the original written consent may have authorised such further treatment as the doctor considered necessary or desirable in the circumstances. Such a wording, if present, would appear to cover the removal of the appendix.

Did Hilda impliedly consent to the removal of her appendix in the circumstances?
Consent to a course of medical treatment can sometimes be implied from the claimant's conduct, eg where a patient holds out her arm in order to receive an injection. It is clearly much more difficult to imply such consent if a patient is unconscious when the need for a consent first arises. It might be thought that the courts would approach the issue on the basis of whether a reasonable person would have wanted their appendix removed during an operation for some other matter, given that it's removal would have been inevitable at some stage in the future. This would obviously depend upon whether any additional risks were involved. However, the courts prefer to approach these questions according to the defence of necessity rather than upon issues of implied consent (*F v West Berkshire Area Health Authority*), and it is submitted that this is the likely basis on which the hospital would have to justify their actions.

Can the removal of the appendix be justified by the defence of necessity?
It has already been noted that that a doctor would be justified in administering urgent, necessary medical treatment where a patient is unconscious and not known to object to it. However, this exception appears to be confined to cases where immediate action is necessary to preserve life or prevent permanent damage to health. It is clear that Hilda's

diseased appendix does not pose any immediate threat to her health, and on this basis, it is submitted that she ought to have been given the opportunity to provide her consent to the procedure, even if that meant a further operation.

There does not appear to be any explicit UK authority on whether consent to one medical procedure justifies another. Whilst the issue was considered by the Canadian courts in *Marshall v Curry* (10) and *Murray v McMurchy* (11) (and resolved as suggested above), the question was expressly left open in *F v West Berkshire Area Health Authority* by Lord Goff. It is submitted that necessity will be no defence in the circumstances described.

References

(1)   (1999) The Times 30 November
(2)   [1971] Ch 734
(3)   [1987] QB 339
(4)   [1911] AC 355
(5)   [1985] 2 All ER 985
(6)   (1609) 12 Co Rep 63
(7)   [1989] 2 All ER 545
(8)   [1997] 147 NLJ 600
(9)   [1995] Fam 127
(10) [1933] 3 DLR 260
(11) [1949] 2 DLR 442

Examination Paper

University of London

LLB Examination June 1999

Law of Tort

Zone A Examination Paper

Time allowed: **three** hours.
Answer **four** of the following **eight** questions.

1. 'We do not for an instant doubt that the common convenience and welfare of a modern plural democracy such as ours are best served by an ample flow of information to the public concerning, and by vigorous public discussion of, matters of public interest to the community.' (*Reynolds* v *Times Newspapers* (1998).)
   Discuss. To what extent is the English law of defamation consistent with that view?

2. Milly required major heart surgery. The operation was performed by Nora, a leading heart surgeon. She decided to use a new technique which avoided some of the risks of conventional surgery. It had never been performed in the United Kingdom, but Nora had observed it carried out in the United States. Nora told Milly how the operation would be performed, but not that it was a new technique. Although the operation was performed with reasonable care, Milly suffered brain damage. She is now severely disabled, unable to work and requires a great deal of care.
   Milly was 22, had just obtained a degree in computer engineering and was about to undertake a graduate degree. Her mother Olivia, who is aged 45, and was a partner in a firm of city solicitors, has given up work to help care for her.
   Advise (a) as to any claims in tort, (b) as to the assessment of damages and (c) as to the advantages and disadvantages of a structured settlement.

3. '... in *Henderson* v *Merrett Syndicates Ltd*, it was settled that the assumption of responsibility principle enunciated in the *Hedley Byrne* case is not confined to statements but may apply to any assumption of responsibility for the provision of services.' (*Williams* v *Natural Life Health Foods Ltd* (1998) per Lord Steyn.)
   Discuss this statement and comment on the use of the concept of 'assumption of responsibility' as the basis of liability.

4. A party of schoolchildren from London went on a week's adventure holiday in Devon. One afternoon they went on a river expedition organised by Titanic Cruises. Twelve of the children were on a boat piloted by Amos, an employee of Titanic Cruises. As the boat approached a dangerous section of river, the steering mechanism failed and Amos was unable to stop the boat being carried towards a weir. The boat crashed over and everyone was thrown overboard and carried down by a raging current. Bianca was standing on the

Law of Tort – June 1999

bank. She tried to climb down the bank but saw at once that she would herself be carried away. She watched helplessly as the children were carried past. Most children were drowned, but two together with Amos were rescued. News of the tragedy was given on the evening news bulletin together with an emergency contact number in Exeter. Cleo telephoned the number from London to ask about her daughter Daphne, who had been on the expedition, and was told that Daphne had drowned. This was a mistake; Daphne had not been on the trip that afternoon.

Amos, Bianca and Cleo have all suffered psychiatric injury. Advise them.

5. Veronique works as an au pair with the Brown family. One evening when the Browns are out, she invites her friend Lucille to visit her. Lucille works as an au pair with another family. Lucille mentions that she has been unable to find a spare part for her old motor scooter. Veronique says that she is sure Mr Brown may have something in his workshop in the garden and that he will not mind if she has a look. Veronique takes Lucille out to the workshop. A substantial quantity of oil has been spilled on the floor of the workshop and Lucille falls over and cuts her arm very badly. Veronique takes Lucille to the local hospital in her car. On the way there is an accident caused by the negligent driving of Giles. Lucille suffers serious leg injuries. The arm injury does not respond to treatment and it has to be amputated.

    Advise Lucille.

6. The (fictitious) Industrial Premises (Alcohol Restriction) Regulations 1999 provide: 'No alcoholic substance shall be taken into or consumed within any premises to which these regulations apply.' The regulations apply to the premises of Goat & Sheep Ltd. Alf, who works at Goat & Sheep, buys four bottles of wine at lunchtime, brings them back to work and places them in a bag on top of the cabinet in the recreation room. During the lunch break, Bill and Clive, who also work at Goat & Sheep, and Des, a lorry driver who has been delivering supplies there, are sitting in the recreation room throwing a frisbee to each other. When Bill throws the frisbee, it strikes the bag containing the wine bottles. They are shattered; broken glass falls on Clive and Des, who are cut, and each of them loses an eye.

    Advise Clive and Des.

7. Gina is a qualified word processor who is registered with Paperjam, a word processing agency. She is at present working at Macro & Merge Ltd, who have recruited her through Paperjam to cover for a member of staff on sick leave. On returning from lunch one day, she saw a man, whom she did not know, alone in the office loading computers onto a trolley. She struck him in the stomach, winding him and ran out locking the office door. The man was Hugo, who was employed by the maintenance department of Macro & Merge, and he was removing the computers in the course of his work. Hugo was known to his employers to suffer from asthma and to be prone to blackouts during which he sometimes needed assistance. Hugo had a very severe asthmatic attack and passed out. He has suffered permanent damage to his health.

    Advise Hugo as to any claims in tort.

8. Ronald leased a small country house from Percival. With Percival's consent, he assigned the unexpired two years of the lease to Stewart in 1998. A shed in the garden contained a considerable amount of rubbish including some paint tins. Stewart did not want to use the shed, did not ask Ronald to remove the rubbish and did not investigate what was there. The paint tins had in fact been used to store a highly corrosive chemical. It has now destroyed the containers and seeped into the adjoining property of Terence. It has made it impossible to grow flowers in a large part of Terence's garden and has destroyed his prize sunflowers. Stewart has disposed of the paint tins but says that he cannot do anything about the chemical which has seeped into the soil. Terence knows that Stewart always likes to watch the 'Newsnight' programme at 10.30 each evening on television and Terence always uses electrical equipment at the time in order to interfere with reception. Ronald's present whereabouts are unknown.

Advise the parties.

Suggested Solutions

Question One

'We do not for an instant doubt that the common convenience and welfare of a modern plural democracy such as ours are best served by an ample flow of information to the public concerning, and by vigorous public discussion of, matters of public interest to the community.' (*Reynolds* v *Times Newspapers* (1998).)

Discuss. To what extent is the English law of defamation consistent with that view?

Suggested Solution

General Comment

Candidates should have avoided a general discussion of the elements of defamation in this question, instead concentrating on the conflict between the need for freedom of expression and the need for the law to protect individual reputations. Discussion concerning the extent to which the law of defamation protects free speech should have concentrated on the defences to an action in defamation, including that of qualified privilege which was the subject of the appeal in the *Reynolds* case. Since this question was set, *Reynolds* has been the subject of a further appeal to the House of Lords, and it is that judgement which is subject to analysis and comment below. The judgment of Lord Nicholls in particular is essential reading for candidates in this area.

Skeleton Solution

Explain that the question is about the conflicting interests of free expression and the need to protect individual reputations – briefly discuss the tort of defamation as a prima facie restriction on the freedom of expression – explain how the law seeks to redress the balance, ie by placing restrictions upon those who can sue and the defences available in a defamation action, those being justification, fair comment and privilege (explain the defences with particular reference to the promotion of free speech) – explain the approach adopted in other jurisdictions to whether political discussion enjoys qualified privilege – discuss the *Reynolds* case and the extent to which the decision upholds freedom of expression, making reference to the position under the European Convention and the Human Rights Act 1998.

Suggested Solution

The quote refers to the need for freedom of expression, and in the context of the House of Lord's decision in *Reynolds* v *Times Newspapers Ltd* (1) it was the expression and communication of information concerning political matters which was in issue.

The tort of defamation represents a restriction on the freedom of expression by recognising the need to protect individual reputations in certain circumstances. The publication of a statement which adversely affects a person's reputation is a defamation, and may be subject to civil proceedings. The claimant need not prove that the allegations were false. Nor must he prove that he suffered damage, provided that the publication was in written or permanent form. However, it should not be supposed that the need to protect individual reputations is a matter of merely personal interest. In *Reynolds*, Lord Nicholls underlined the importance of personal reputation and commented:

> 'It is in the public interest that the reputation of public figures should not be debased falsely. In the political field, in order to make an informed choice, the electorate needs to be able to identify the good as well as the bad.'

In providing a right of redress to those who have unjustifiably suffered damage to their reputations by the publication of defamatory material, the law does, however, seek to balance individual interests against the general interests of a democratic society by ensuring free speech. The law achieves such a balance in two ways: by preventing some types of potential claimant from bringing actions in defamation, and by providing a range of defences to those who are alleged to have published defamatory material. Each of these will be dealt with in turn.

Restrictions upon those who may bring actions in defamation
In *Derbyshire County Council* v *Times Newspapers Ltd* (2) the House of Lords held that local authorities, as democratically elected government bodies, and central government departments, which are statutory corporations, must be open to uninhibited public criticism, and are therefore not entitled to bring a claim in defamation. Individual councillors who have been defamed may bring actions in their own name, but the only legitimate response of a local council which is subject to public criticism is to defend itself by public utterances and by debate in the local council chamber.

This decision clearly upholds the principle of freedom of expression as regards actions (or lack of action) taken by local authorities and central government departments.

Defences
A range of defences exist to protect defendants from defamation actions in certain circumstances, thus in theory upholding and encouraging the principle of freedom of expression. The defendant may, of course, establish that the allegations were true. However, this alone is not enough to encourage free speech: the difficulties of proving the truth of every allegation, and the fear and uncertainty of expensive litigation, would have a chilling effect, discouraging the publication of potentially important material. Thus, defences have also been developed at common law which allow for honest opinions to be expressed on matters of public interest, and for statements to be made on privileged occasions, even though honest factual mistakes were made.

Justification
If the defendant can prove that the substance of the statement was true, then he has a complete defence (*Alexander* v *North Eastern Railway Co* (3)), even if he was acting spitefully in publishing the statement.

Fair comment
The defence of fair comment is frequently invoked by the courts, especially by the press, and along with qualified privilege is one of the defences which is important in establishing the limits of free speech in this country. Indeed, Lord Nicholls in *Reynolds* stated that 'the freedom of expression protected by this defence has long been regarded by the common law as a basic right, long before the emergence of human rights Conventions.' The defendant must show that the matter to which the statement referred was one of public interest, that his comment was an opinion based upon true facts (which were explicitly or implicitly identified in the publication, at least in general terms), that the comment was fair and that it was made without malice.

That freedom of expression is promoted by this defence may be illustrated by reference to the broad manner in which some of the elements are defined. A matter is said to be in the public interest whenever it 'is such as to affect people at large, so that they may legitimately be interested in, or concerned at, what is going on; or what may happen to them or others': *London Artists Ltd v Littler* (4) per Lord Denning.

As to whether the comment is 'fair' Lord Nicholls in *Reynolds* stated:

> 'Judges have emphasised the latitude to be applied in interpreting this standard. So much so that the time has come to recognise that in this context the epithet "fair" is now meaningless and misleading ... the basis of our public life is that the crank, the enthusiast, may say what he honestly thinks as much as the reasonable person who sits on a jury. The true test is whether the opinion, however exaggerated, obstinate or prejudiced, was honestly held by the person expressing it.'

Privilege
This defence recognises that, in certain circumstances, it is particularly important to encourage the free and uninhibited communication of particular information from particular sources. This is achieved either by providing a blanket immunity from things published on particular occasions (absolute privilege), eg statements made in Parliament, or by judges, counsel, parties or witnesses during judicial proceedings, or by protecting what is published from liability unless the claimant can prove that the defendant was actuated by malice (qualified privilege).

A number of occasions benefiting from qualified privilege have been identified by the courts and by Parliament. For example, fair and accurate reporting of the public proceedings of legislatures, courts and public enquiries worldwide are subject to qualified privilege under the Defamation Act 1996.

However, the courts do not regard these categories of 'occasions' as being closed. In *Adam v Ward* (5) Lord Atkinson stated:

> '... a privileged occasion is ... an occasion where the person who makes a communication has an interest or a duty, legal, social or moral, to make it to the person to whom it is made, and the person to whom it is made has a corresponding interest or duty to receive it. This reciprocity is essential.'

The occasions on which a qualified privilege may arise are therefore potentially wide, and there will be freedom of expression in these circumstances unless the publisher of the statement was actuated by malice. The burden of proof falls upon the claimant on these occasions to prove that the defendant was malicious. Such a burden will often be difficult to discharge, and will involve proving that the defendant had no honest belief in the truth of his statement, or that the defendant used the occasion for some reason other than that for which the privileged existed: *Horrocks v Lowe* (6).

Qualified privilege and the publication of political discussion in the media
Some common law jurisdictions have gone so far as to recognise a generic category of qualified privilege in respect of political discussion. Such recognition tips the balance in favour of the freedom of expression, as there is no initial presumption of defamation in the case of a politician who has been the subject of adverse comment in the media. This might be thought unfair given that the widespread dissemination of defamatory material is potentially extremely damaging to those in the public eye.

In the United States, recognition of a 'public figure' defence occurred in the case of *New York Times Co v Sullivan* (7). A public official cannot recover damages for defamation relating to his official conduct unless he proves that the statement was knowingly false or made with reckless disregard as to its accuracy. A plaintiff is entitled to a pre-trial inquiry into a newspaper's sources and the editorial decision-making process.

In Australia, the High Court in *Lange v Australian Broadcasting Corporation* (8) held that qualified privilege automatically exists in respect of the dissemination of information, opinions and arguments concerning government and political matters, subject only to a requirement of due care. Precise guidelines were laid down as to the steps required of publishers to satisfy the requirements of due care. A publisher must not only believe that the imputation was true, but must also take reasonable steps to verify the accuracy of the information and must seek and publish a response from the individual defamed, where practicable.

Reynolds *v* Times Newspapers Ltd
This case was brought by the former Irish Prime Minister, Albert Reynolds, following his resignation on the collapse of the coalition government in 1994. An article in the *Sunday Times* alleged that he had lied to the Irish Parliament and to his coalition colleagues. The story was of interest to a British readership, as Reynolds had been one of the chief architects of the Northern Ireland peace agreement. The article proved to be factually false even though it had been honestly made. The main issue before the House of Lords was whether the newspaper were entitled to rely on the defence of qualified privilege. Counsel for Times Newspapers invited the House to consider developing a new category of qualified privilege to cover the publication of political information, in line with the approach adopted in Australia.

Consequences for the protection of personal reputation
The leading judgement was that of Lord Nicholls, who underlined the importance of personal reputation:

> 'Reputation is an integral and important part of the dignity of the individual. It also forms the basis of many decisions in a democratic society which are fundamental to its well-being: whom to employ or work for, whom to promote, whom to do business with or to vote for. Once besmirched by an unfounded allegation in a national newspaper, a reputation can be damaged forever, especially if there is no opportunity to vindicate one's reputation.'

Their Lordships refused to establish a new generic category of qualified privilege based upon the publication of political information, as it was thought that this would not provide adequate protection for the reputation of politicians: it would be extremely difficult for a political figure to prove malice without discovering the newspaper's sources, which are largely protected by s10 Contempt of Court Act 1981. Contrast this with the position in the US, where a public figure is entitled to a pre-trial enquiry to discover sources and details of the editorial decision-making process. Their Lordships also pointed out that it was inconsistent to provide protection as regards political discussion but not in respect of other matters of serious public concern, given that certain non-political public figures exercise great practical influence.

A recurring theme throughout the judgements was the suspicion that any blanket privilege would be subject to abuse by the press given the commercial pressures to publish scoops and the temptation to exaggerate or distort facts to excite the interest of readers. Lord Nicholls in particular noted that the self-regulation of the press had not always been a success.

Lord Nicholls upheld the traditional duty/interest test outlined in *Adam v Ward*, stating that the question of whether the public were entitled to know political or other information was a question to be determined by a judge considering all the circumstances of the publication. He put forward ten non-inclusive factors which might be considered when determining whether the duty/interest test would be satisfied, including the seriousness of the allegation, the nature and source of the information, the steps taken to verify it, whether comment was sought from the claimant and whether the article contained the gist of the claimant's version of events. An approach to determining the existence of qualified privilege which involves balancing the competing interests of the parties on a case-by-case basis according to the individual facts would accord with the approach and jurisprudence of the European Court of Human Rights.

On the facts, The Times were unable to establish the defence of qualified privilege, as their failure to seek or to publish Mr Reynold's explanation of events meant that the public had no right to know the information concerned.

Consequences for the protection of freedom of expression
We have seen that the defences available to an action in defamation go some way towards protecting the rights of those who engage in honest political reporting and discussion, at least where the subject matter can be said to relate to the public interest. The decision in *Reynolds* relating to qualified privilege seems to uphold the interests of individual reputations at the expense of freedom of expression. However, this is far from being the true effect of their Lordships' decision. Freedom of expression is now the starting point for the consideration of any claim for qualified privilege by the media, and the courts are instructed to pay particular regard to the vital functions discharged by the press in acting as both 'bloodhound' and 'watchdog'. Lord Nicholls stated that courts should be reluctant to conclude that an article involving political discussion is not in the public interest: any doubts should be resolved in favour of publication. Lord Steyn even suggested at one point that the press have a general duty to inform the public on political matters and that the public has a right to be informed. However, their Lordships ultimately favoured a case-by-case approach to this question. Lord Nicholls affirmed that any unwillingness on the part of

newspapers to disclose their sources should not weigh against them when determining the duty/interest test.

The approach of the House is consistent with s12 Human Rights Act 1998 which requires the courts to pay particular regard to the importance of freedom of expression. The law regarding political discussion (and indeed other matters of public concern) has now moved closer to the Australian approach in *Lange*, without the establishment of any new generic category of qualified privilege or precisely defined public interest criteria. It is likely that the courts will, in future, find that qualified privilege exists in cases where reasonable and responsible standards of journalism have been adhered to.

References

(1) [1999] 4 All ER 609
(2) [1993] 2 WLR 449
(3) (1865) 6 B & S 340
(4) [1969] 2 QB 375
(5) [1917] AC 309
(6) [1975] AC 135
(7) (1964) 376 US 254 (US SC)
(8) (1997) 145 ALR 96

Question Two

Milly required major heart surgery. The operation was performed by Nora, a leading heart surgeon. She decided to use a new technique which avoided some of the risks of conventional surgery. It had never been performed in the United Kingdom, but Nora had observed it carried out in the United States. Nora told Milly how the operation would be performed, but not that it was a new technique. Although the operation was performed with reasonable care, Milly suffered brain damage. She is now severely disabled, unable to work and requires a great deal of care.

Milly was 22, had just obtained a degree in computer engineering and was about to undertake a graduate degree. Her mother Olivia, who is aged 45, and was a partner in a firm of city solicitors, has given up work to help care for her.

Advise (a) as to any claims in tort, (b) as to the assessment of damages and (c) as to the advantages and disadvantages of a structured settlement.

Suggested Solution

General Comment

This question was relatively straightforward, provided candidates had revised remedies as well as substantive liability. Candidates should have avoided any detailed examination of elements of negligence which were not in issue, such as whether a duty of care existed in this case. When discussing the advantages and disadvantages of structured settlements, do make sure that the points you raise are fully explained.

Skeleton Solution

a) Discuss Nora's liability in the tort of negligence, in particular the scope of the duty to disclose the risks involved in surgery under *Sidaway*, *Bolam* and *Bolitho* – discuss whether a breach of any duty by Nora caused Milly's loss.
b) Identify the aim of damages in tort and explain the heads of loss relevant to Milly's circumstances, under which damages will be assessed – make particular reference to future loss of earnings, and the provision of care by a relative.
c) Explain the nature of structured settlements, their advantages and disadvantages.

Suggested Solution

a) *Nora's liability in tort*

If Milly is to claim against Nora in tort, such a claim will be based in negligen'

Nora's duty to give her patient proper and skilled advice, rather than in trespass as a battery which lacks the patient's valid consent. Only if Nora had actively misled Milly concerning the fact that she was unpractised in the new technique for performing heart surgery would an action in battery be likely to arise: *Sidaway v Bethlem Royal Hospital Governors* (1).

It is well established that doctors owe duties of care to their patients, not only in the context of diagnosis and treatment, but also (in limited circumstances) to disclose the risks involved in a course of treatment. This was confirmed by the House of Lords in *Sidaway* and subsequently by the Court of Appeal in *Gold v Haringey Health Authority* (2).

In order to determine whether Nora is in breach of her duty to Milly, it is necessary to examine the scope of the duty she owes. The majority of their Lordships in *Sidaway* held that the proper test to apply in these circumstances is that established in *Bolam v Friern Hospital Management Committee* (3); in other words, the test is whether a reasonable doctor would have acted as the defendant had done. A doctor will be held to have acted reasonably if he acted in accordance with a practice accepted as proper by a responsible body of medical men skilled in that particular art. Not only would Nora's failure to inform Milly that she intended to use a new technique (with which she had no previous 'hands on' experience) have to accord with a practice accepted as proper by a responsible body of doctors, the court would also have to be satisfied that this practice of non-disclosure has a logical basis: *Bolitho v City and Hackney Health Authority* (4).

It would obviously be rare to find that a body of professional opinion lacked logical analysis. Lord Browne-Wilkinson in *Bolitho* said that a judge would not normally be able to draw such a conclusion without expert evidence, and if the body of opinion reflected an accepted practice in the profession, a judge would not be able to discard that practice unless it could not be logically supported at all.

It is difficult to speculate whether Nora's non-disclosure was in accordance with the commonly accepted practice of a body of responsible doctors. Nora did, after all, explain how the operation would be performed. One body of professional opinion might logically consider that such a disclosure would inhibit the introduction of new and unpractised procedures, as few patients might consent if they were aware that they were the first to be subjected to a new procedure. On the other hand, the court might conclude that it is illogical to assume that patients would not consent to a new procedure which offers a clear reduction in risks compared to conventional surgery.

It should be noted that the minority of their Lordships in *Sidaway* held that the disclosure of some risks are so obviously necessary to an informed choice on the part of a patient that no reasonable prudent medical man would fail to make them. The information not disclosed in this case might well be regarded as essential to allow a patient to make an informed choice; however, it is the view of the majority which has been followed in later cases. As such, there is no duty on the part of doctors to enable patients to make an informed choice in English law.

Assuming Nora were to have broken a duty of disclosure to Milly, it would also have to be proved that 'but for' the non-disclosure, Milly would not have consented to the new technique, and would not thereby have suffered brain damage: *Barnett v Chelsea and Kensington Hospital Management Committee* (5).

b) *The assessment of damages*
Assuming Nora is in breach of a duty of care owed to Milly, Nora's employer will be vicariously liable to pay a lump sum of damages (unless the parties were to agree to a structured settlement: see (c) below). The aim of such an award will be to restore Milly, in so far as money will allow, to the position she was in before the negligence occurred. An award of damages is usually considered in two parts: 'special damages' covering precisely calculable losses, normally arising pre-trial, and 'general damages' which are not capable of precise mathematical calculation and normally arise post-trial. It is also customary to classify losses sustained as being either pecuniary or non-pecuniary.

Pecuniary losses: loss of earnings
These mostly arise post-trial in Milly's case, and will include prospective earnings during any 'lost years' due to a reduced life expectancy and loss of pension rights associated with a future loss of salary.

Milly's future loss of salary is clearly difficult to assess as she has not yet entered the job market. It is likely that, had Milly become fully qualified, she would have been extremely employable and would have attracted a high salary. The court will award Milly a lump sum which, when invested, will be sufficient to produce an income equal to the loss of her future salary. The calculation is approached in two stages. The court will first assess Milly's net annual loss. The difficulty here is knowing how much Milly would have earned upon her entry to the job market (as a computer engineer?). Nonetheless, the court will have to make some assumptions, most probably based upon evidence from someone with expert knowledge of Milly's future intended profession.

The court will then select a multiplier based upon the likely duration of the disability. However, this will not be the same as the number of years Milly will work before retirement following completion of her post-graduate course, because the courts apply a reduction to take account of the possibility that future events might have cut her working life short, eg early death or unemployment. The possibility that Milly might have taken a career break for several years in order to raise children will also be a limiting factor. A reduction is also applied to take account of the fact that a lump sum payment will produce an investment income of its own. Other factors, such as Milly's future promotion prospects, may well increase the multiplier. This factor, together with Milly's young age, means that she is likely to obtain a near-maximum multiplier, perhaps in the range of 16–18.

Medical expenses reasonably incurred
The cost of nursing care and travel expenses to and from hospital are recoverable. The cost of nursing care provided by Olivia can be recovered by Milly herself: *Hunt* v *Severs* (6). In *Housecroft* v *Burnett* (7) it was decided that where a relative gives up work to look after the claimant, the court will award reasonable recompense to the carer, but the ceiling on such an award is the commercial rate for providing such care. Thus Olivia will be unable to recover her full loss of earnings, given her former employment as a partner in a city firm of solicitors. The damages awarded in respect of the carer will be held on trust for Olivia by Milly: *Cunningham* v *Harrison* (8).

Non-pecuniary losses

Milly's non-pecuniary losses include the pain and suffering she has endured both pre and post-trial, her loss of amenity, ie the loss of capacity to engage in activities which she enjoyed before trial, and compensation for her actual injuries. The amounts awarded under these heads are usually assessed by reference to past cases.

c) *The structured settlement*

This type of settlement was developed following pressure from those involved in clinical negligence claims (eg lawyers and insurers) and from tax concessions made by the Inland Revenue. The Damages Act 1996 provided further statutory support. Structured settlements may be suitable in cases such as Milly's where substantial damages are payable, but they can only be made where both parties agree.

Once a lump sum figure has been agreed, the part of the award representing special damages to the date of settlement would be paid to Milly as a lump sum. The remainder is used by the defendant's insurers to purchase an annuity to provide a fixed income stream for the claimant. Variations in payments from the annuity can be built in to cater for various contingencies likely to arise during the life of the claimant.

Advantages of structured settlements
1. Income from the annuity is tax free (benefiting higher rate taxpayers in particular) whereas income from the investment of a lump sum will be subject to income tax. Thus income payments from a structured settlement are likely to be larger.
2. A structured settlement would provide certainty for Milly in respect of her future income, and would avoid the danger that a lump sum might be spent too quickly, leaving insufficient funds for later years.
3. Milly is quite possibly unable to manage the investment of a lump sum herself given the extent of her disabilities, and would be reliant on the goodwill, good faith, and investment expertise of those who care for her to manage her affairs. The use of a structured settlement removes this responsibility from the claimant.
4. Annuities can be set up to protect future income from the effects of inflation.
5. The income from an annuity will be guaranteed to last for Milly's lifetime, even if she survived longer than her predicted life expectancy.

Disadvantages of structured settlements
1. Even though there is flexibility within a structured settlement to vary payments to cater for various contingencies likely to arise during the life of the claimant, once agreed, a structured settlement cannot be modified. This means that there is extreme pressure to structure the settlement correctly at the outset. Predictions concerning Milly's future need for income and capital will have to be made straight away.
2. The amounts payable under a structured settlement may still be inadequate if Milly's prognosis is incorrect.

References

(1) [1985] AC 871
(2) [1988] QB 481

References (contd.)

(3) [1957] 1 WLR 582
(4) [1997] 4 All ER 771
(5) [1969] 1 QB 428
(6) [1994] 2 All ER 385
(7) [1986] 1 All ER 332
(8) [1973] QB 942

Question Three

'... in *Henderson* v *Merrett Syndicates Ltd*, it was settled that the assumption of responsibility principle enunciated in the *Hedley Byrne* case is not confined to statements but may apply to any assumption of responsibility for the provision of services.' (*Williams* v *Natural Life Health Foods Ltd* (1998) per Lord Steyn.)

Discuss this statement and comment on the use of the concept of 'assumption of responsibility' as the basis of liability.

Suggested Solution

General Comment

This question would have suited those candidates who were keeping themselves fully up-to-date with current developments in tortious liability in the House of Lords. Such contemporary developments are always possible areas for examination (see also Question One), although a more in-depth analysis and comment upon the law will usually be required to compensate for predictability. Candidates should have concentrated their efforts on describing recent case law concerning liability for the provision of services, rather than the historical development of the *Hedley Byrne* principles relating to negligent misstatements. The two cases mentioned in the question were obvious starting points.

Skeleton Solution

Describe the notion of 'assumption of responsibility' as a criterion for liability in respect of negligent statements under *Hedley Byrne* – explain how the concept has been used to extend liability to the provision of services – discuss specific examples, in particular *Henderson*; *White* v *Jones*; *Williams* – criticise the concept of 'assumption of responsibility' as a basis for liability, describing the different attitudes of the judges to it.

Suggested Solution

In *Hedley Byrne & Co Ltd* v *Heller & Partners Ltd* (1) the House of Lords established that pure economic loss, suffered as a consequence of reasonable reliance by the claimant upon the defendant's negligent statement, is recoverable.

All of their Lordships justified their decisions upon the basis of one party having assumed a responsibility towards the other. Lord Devlin in particular held that the 'special relationship' necessary for a duty of care to arise occurred in relationships which '... are equivalent to contract'; that is, there is an assumption of responsibility in circumstances in which, but for the absence of consideration, there would be a contract.' Lord Devlin also stated: 'Cases may arise in the future in which a new and wider proposition, quite independent of any notion of contract, will be needed.'

This essay will concentrate on how notions of 'assumption of responsibility' have been used by the courts since *Hedley Byrne* to extend the principles established in that case to the negligent performance of services in addition to negligent statements and advice. Such extensions were made in order to do individual justice in cases where the claimants concerned had suffered pure economic loss, and would therefore have been unable to recover under normal negligence principles.

The extension of the Hedley Byrne principle to the provision of services
A suggestion that *Hedley Byrne* was not simply to be confined to 'statement' cases came in the judgements of Lord Oliver in *D & F Estates Ltd* v *The Church Commissioners for England* (2) and Lord Keith in *Murphy* v *Brentwood District Council* (3). Their Lordships classified the decision of the House of Lords in *Junior Books Ltd* v *The Veitchi Co Ltd* (4) as an example of *Hedley Byrne*-type liability. However, *Junior Books* was a case concerning the recovery for economic loss arising from a defective product rather than a negligent statement.

The extension of *Hedley Byrne* principles to cover negligently provided services is, perhaps, unsurprising. Many professional services are based wholly or partly upon the giving of advice. A significant extension of liability eventually occurred in *Henderson* v *Merrett Syndicates Ltd* (5), a case arising out of the losses suffered by Lloyd's 'names' following advice given by their underwriting agents as to the risks involved. The House of Lords decided that a duty of care would exist where a person assumed responsibility to perform professional or quasi-professional services for another who relied on those services. Lord Goff stated:

> '... though *Hedley Byrne* was concerned with the provision of information and advice, the example given by Lord Devlin ... and his and Lord Morris's statement of principle show that the principle extends beyond the provision of information and advice to include the performance of other services.'

The scope of this extended duty will necessarily be limited, because service providers are only likely to assume responsibility to specific individuals, or to a limited class of specific recipients, in respect of their services. Thus, liability can be maintained within acceptable bounds.

Similarly, in *White* v *Jones* (6) Lords Goff and Browne-Wilkinson applied *Hedley Byrne* in order to impose liability upon a solicitor who had negligently failed to carry out instructions in preparing a new will, resulting in financial loss to the intended beneficiaries. The lack of privity of contract between the solicitors and beneficiaries did not prevent a claim in negligence, because a 'special relationship' arose between the parties, the defendant having assumed a responsibility for the economic welfare of the beneficiaries. A point of particular difficulty in this case was that the beneficiaries could not necessarily be said to have relied upon the defendant's expertise as a matter of fact, given that beneficiaries are usually unaware of the provisions which have been made for them in a will. However, in order to allow the beneficiaries a claim, their Lordships held that reliance is not a necessary condition for the creation of a 'special relationship' in every case under the extended *Hedley Byrne* principle.

White v *Jones* therefore, clearly indicates that *Hedley Byrne* principles may be extended to the provision of services, even if those services were provided at the request of a third party.

The case of *Williams* v *Natural Life Health Foods Ltd* (7) involved a claim for substantial economic losses following the failure of a franchisee's natural health business. It was claimed that the loss arose from negligent advice provided by the franchisor, a company run by the defendant (who was the principal shareholder and managing director). However, the franchisor had been wound-up and dissolved, and so the claimants sued the defendant, attempting to prove that he had personally assumed responsibility for the negligent advice. On the facts, the House of Lords held that the defendant had not assumed personal responsibility for the advice and the claim failed.

Lord Steyn confirmed that 'assumption of responsibility' is the basis for liability under the extended *Hedley Byrne* doctrine. The test is an objective one, not depending upon the state of mind of the defendant but upon evidence of statements or conduct which conveyed to the claimants that the defendant was willing to assume personal responsibility for them. Lord Steyn held that reliance by the claimants on the assumption of responsibility is necessary to establish causation. However, the test is not whether, in fact, the claimant relied upon the assumption of responsibility, but whether it was reasonable to rely on the defendant to take personal responsibility in all the circumstances.

Thus it can be seen that recovery for pure economic loss arising from the negligent provision of services is now possible under English law. The *Hedley Byrne* test as applied to negligent misstatements has, by necessity, been adapted to apply more easily to the provision of services. For example, reliance by the claimant, as a question of fact, could not be established in many situations involving the provision of services.

The concept of 'assumption of responsibility' as the basis of liability
It was once thought that the 'assumption of responsibility' test was nothing more than a convenient phrase to describe the situation in which a duty of care would be recognised or imposed by the law. In *Caparo Industries Ltd plc* v *Dickman* (8) Lord Oliver stated that 'it was not intended to be a test for the existence of the duty ... It tells us nothing about the circumstances from which such attribution arises.' However, as we have seen, there have been attempts to adapt the test as a criterion for liability in the recent cases concerning pure economic loss arising from the provision of services.

One criticism of the current concept of 'assumption of responsibility' as a test for liability is that it is too uncertain and imprecise to provide useful guidance to trial judges in future cases. As such, it could simply be used as a tool to justify a finding of liability when the court feels that the justice of the situation requires such a conclusion. This makes it hard for lawyers advising the parties to predict the outcome of a dispute, thus possibly necessitating expensive litigation.

There is evidence supporting the view that the concept might simply be used as a tool to justify liability in the authorities already discussed. In *White* v *Jones* Lord Goff openly admitted that he was motivated to achieve practical justice, because a lack of privity of contract would have denied the beneficiaries a claim. The testator's estate had suffered no loss and so a claim for breach of contract would not have been sustainable on the facts. The defendants would escape liability for their admitted negligence unless the court was prepared to impose a concurrent duty in tort.

The formulation of 'assumption of responsibility' by Lord Steyn in *Williams* is also unsatisfactory in that it cannot explain all the cases. For example, in *Smith v Eric S Bush (A Firm)* (9) the defendant surveyors, instructed by a building society, had sought to avoid liability to the claimant house purchaser by the use of a disclaimer. Nonetheless, the claimant was held to be entitled to rely upon the valuer's report, even though the disclaimer said that the survey was prepared for the benefit of the building society and not the claimant. Surely, it could not be said that the surveyor had shown a willingness to assume a personal responsibility to the house purchaser by statements or conduct, given the clear wording of the disclaimer? Lord Steyn regarded *Smith v Bush* as an awkward case decided on special facts, which was very much based on the need to 'yield to practical justice'.

Perhaps a more coherent version of the 'assumption of responsibility' is that formulated by Lord Browne-Wilkinson in *White v Jones*. This would involve liability based upon 'a conscious assumption of responsibility for the task' which benefits the claimant, rather than 'a conscious assumption of legal responsibility to the plaintiff for its careful performance.' Such a formulation would avoid the difficulties associated with Lord Steyn's approach when it comes to explaining cases such as *Smith v Bush*. Alternatively, it has been suggested that the *Donoghue v Stevenson* (10) conception of proximity, which asks whether the claimant was a person 'so closely and directly affected by my act that I ought reasonably to have them in contemplation', would provide a suitable alternative criterion in cases like these (11).

References

(1) [1964] AC 465
(2) [1989] AC 177
(3) [1990] 3 WLR 414
(4) [1983] 1 AC 520
(5) [1994] 3 WLR 761
(6) [1995] 2 WLR 187
(7) [1998] 2 All ER 577
(8) [1990] 2 AC 605
(9) [1990] 1 AC 831
(10) [1932] AC 562
(11) Cooke, John, *Law of Tort* (4th edn, 1999)

Question Four

A party of schoolchildren from London went on a week's adventure holiday in Devon. One afternoon they went on a river expedition organised by Titanic Cruises. Twelve of the children were on a boat piloted by Amos, an employee of Titanic Cruises. As the boat approached a dangerous section of river, the steering mechanism failed and Amos was unable to stop the boat being carried towards a weir. The boat crashed over and everyone was thrown overboard and carried down by a raging current. Bianca was standing on the bank. She tried to climb down the bank but saw at once that she would herself be carried away. She watched helplessly as the children were carried past. Most children were drowned, but two together with Amos were rescued. News of the tragedy was given on the evening news bulletin together with an emergency contact number in Exeter. Cleo telephoned the number from London to ask about her daughter Daphne, who had been on the expedition, and was told that Daphne had drowned. This was a mistake; Daphne had not been on the trip that afternoon.

Amos, Bianca and Cleo have all suffered psychiatric injury. Advise them.

Suggested Solution

General Comment

This should have been a relatively straightforward question for those candidates who revised the law concerning the recovery of compensation for psychiatric injury, provided they were up to date with the most recent case developments. It must of course be remembered that 'nervous shock' is a type of damage rather than a tort, and therefore candidates would first have needed to identify the basis upon which the defendant might be held liable to those involved in the accident.

Skeleton Solution

Identify and discuss the basis for liability – elements of negligence: duty; breach (res ipsa loquitur); causation; remoteness of damages – discuss each potential claim for recovery in respect of psychiatric illness: Amos as a primary victim; Bianca and Cleo as secondary victims – does Cleo have an alternative claim for a negligent statement made by the Exeter authorities?

Law of Tort – June 1999

Suggested Solution

Basis for liability

It appears that Titanic Cruises may well be liable in negligence to the primary victims of the accident, ie Amos and the children, on the basis of their apparent failure to properly maintain the boat, if indeed this was the case. The elements of the tort of negligence are briefly as follows.

1. The defendant must have owed the claimant a duty of care

    The modern approach for determining whether a duty of care should be imposed in a novel case was recommended by the House of Lords in *Caparo Industries Ltd plc v Dickman* (1). The question is approached in the three stages shown below.

    a) Assuming Titanic had failed to properly maintain the boat, were the consequences of that failure reasonably foreseeable? It would have to be proved that the failure of the steering mechanism was a reasonably foreseeable consequence of a failure to properly maintain the boat. If this were the case, it is submitted that the resulting inability to properly navigate the boat in fast moving rapids would almost inevitably result in a crash, causing injury to the occupants of the boat.

    b) Was the relationship between the defendant and the claimant(s) sufficiently proximate? This requirement is easily satisfied on the facts, because it is the negligent infliction of physical injury which itself appears to create the required degree of proximity.

    c) Would it be 'fair, just and reasonable' in all the circumstances for the courts to impose a duty of care? This requirement is heavily influenced by policy considerations, and it is submitted that it would certainly be fair, just and reasonable to impose a duty of care upon Titanic in these circumstances. Titanic are likely to be insured against claims arising from its business activities, and to allow this type of claim would certainly not result in an opening of the 'floodgates of litigation'. It might be argued that imposing a duty in these circumstances will encourage other similar operators to take care.

2. The defendant must be in breach of that duty

    This involves deciding whether Titanic's conduct fell short of the standard of care which would have been adopted by reasonable persons in the circumstances. The amount of care required in each particular case will depend upon different factors, such as the likelihood of people suffering injury from the hazard, balanced against the practicality of taking precautions in terms of cost and otherwise: *Bolton v Stone* (2). The extent of the potential damage may also be relevant.

    In this case, the maxim 'res ipsa locquitur' (the thing speaks for itself) may apply, as the facts appear to be sufficient to give rise to an inference of negligence on Titanic's part. If such were the case, the court would not require the claimant to give detailed evidence regarding Titanic's failure to maintain the boat. Instead, it would fall to Titanic to rebut the inference of negligence.

    For the maxim to apply, the claimant must show that Titanic was in control of the thing (ie the boat) which caused the loss or damage, and that the accident was of such a nature that it would not have occurred in the ordinary course of events with proper care. It might be suggested that a steering defect would have been unlikely to occur had the boat been properly maintained. Finally, the cause of the accident must be unknown in that it cannot be easily explained. This criterion may apply assuming that no cause can readily be advanced for the failure of the steering mechanism.

3. The breach of duty must have caused the claimant to suffer reasonably foreseeable damage/loss
Assuming that the failure of the steering mechanism resulted from a breach of a duty owed by Titanic, there can be no doubt that the deaths of the children and the psychiatric injuries suffered by the various claimants were direct factual causes. The question as to whether the psychiatric injuries were reasonably foreseeable is dealt with below. The following analysis assumes that Titanic were negligent in respect of physical harm suffered by Amos and the other primary victims of the accident.

Can Amos recover as a primary victim of the accident?
The law relating to the recovery of compensation for psychiatric illness in tort makes a distinction between primary and secondary victims. Primary victims are those who are physically threatened by the negligence, and either suffer personal injury or are put in fear of suffering injury. A secondary victim is someone who is a witness to the consequences of a negligent act or omission in respect of a primary victim.

Amos is a primary victim as he was directly involved in the accident and must have feared for his own life and/or was an active participant in an accident caused by Titanic's negligence: *Dooley* v *Cammell Laird & Co Ltd* (3). This level of direct involvement in the accident automatically establishes a relationship of proximity between Amos and Titanic. The fact that Amos is Titanic's employee does not automatically give him the status of a primary victim. In *White* v *Chief Constable of South Yorkshire Police* (4) the House of Lords decided that an employer is not under a duty to protect employees from psychiatric injury unless the employer is in breach of a duty to protect employees from physical harm. Assuming that Titanic were negligent in respect of the latter, there is no requirement that Amos' psychiatric injury should have been reasonably foreseeable and Amos will be able to recover compensation accordingly. It does not matter whether or not Amos actually suffered physical injury: it is sufficient that physical harm was reasonably foreseeable in the circumstances, even if psychiatric harm was not: *Page* v *Smith* (5).

Can Bianca recover as a primary victim of the accident?
Bianca is a secondary victim of Titanic's negligence in that she was a mere bystander or witness to the accident rather than an active participant: *Robertson* v *Forth Bridge Joint Board* (6). She was not put in fear for her own safety, as it is for this reason that she desisted in her initial attempts to climb down the bank of the river. Bianca is therefore in the position of having to show, in addition, that her psychiatric injury was a reasonably foreseeable consequence of Titanic's negligence. This will require Bianca to satisfy a number of extra criteria which were first established in the case of *McLoughlin* v *O'Brian* (7) and subsequently refined in *Alcock* v *Chief Constable of South Yorkshire* (8). These criteria have been imposed in order to limit the class of potential claimants in such cases. The criteria are as follows.

1. It must have been reasonably foreseeable that Bianca would suffer psychiatric illness as her relationship with at least one of the primary victims was sufficiently close.

   This would normally require a relationship based upon close ties of love and affection between the claimant and the primary victim, comparable to those of a normal parent, spouse or child. Whilst three of the Lords in *Alcock* suggested obiter that claims by unrelated bystanders might not be excluded where a particularly horrific catastrophe occurs within very close range, this suggestion was not subsequently followed by the Court of Appeal in *McFarlane* v *Caledonia Ltd* (9). The Court reasoned that to exclude the requirement of close ties of love and affection between the claimant and primary victim would be to base the test for recovery upon foreseeability alone.

   It is the requirement for a relationship of proximity which almost certainly excludes Bianca's claim in the instant case, given that she appears to be unrelated to any of the primary victims. The other criteria for recovery in *Alcock* would, however, have been satisfied in Bianca's case.
2. The claimant must have been proximate in both time and space to the accident or its immediate aftermath.
3. The psychiatric injury must have been sustained through direct perception of the accident (or its immediate aftermath) with the claimant's own unaided senses.

Can Cleo recover as a secondary victim of the accident?
Any claim by Cleo for psychiatric injury as a secondary victim of Titanic's negligence would certainly be excluded under the aforementioned criteria in *Alcock*. Whilst the relationship between parent and child is one of sufficient proximity (see *McLoughlin*), Cleo was neither close in time and space to the accident or its immediate aftermath, nor did she perceive the events with her own unaided senses. A news report cannot equate with the direct sight or hearing of an event, and being told about an accident does not, by itself, suffice.

However, whilst Cleo might not have a claim against Titanic under the present state of the law, she might have a claim against the Exeter authorities on the basis of their incorrect statement, provided it could be established that they owed a duty of care to callers on the emergency number to take reasonable care to give accurate information.

References

(1) [1990] 2 AC 605
(2) [1951] AC 850
(3) [1951] 1 Lloyd's Rep 271
(4) [1999] 1 All ER 1
(5) [1995] 2 WLR 644
(6) (1995) The Times 13 April
(7) [1983] 1 AC 410
(8) [1992] 1 AC 310
(9) [1994] 2 All ER 1

Question Five

Veronique works as an au pair with the Brown family. One evening when the Browns are out, she invites her friend Lucille to visit her. Lucille works as an au pair with another family. Lucille mentions that she has been unable to find a spare part for her old motor scooter. Veronique says that she is sure Mr Brown may have something in his workshop in the garden and that he will not mind if she has a look. Veronique takes Lucille out to the workshop. A substantial quantity of oil has been spilled on the floor of the workshop and Lucille falls over and cuts her arm very badly. Veronique takes Lucille to the local hospital in her car. On the way there is an accident caused by the negligent driving of Giles. Lucille suffers serious leg injuries. The arm injury does not respond to treatment and it has to be amputated.

Advise Lucille.

Suggested Solution

General Comment

This question concerns the liability of an occupier of defective premises for loss or injury sustained by those who come onto those premises. Any such case should be dealt with as a statutory claim under the Occupiers' Liability Acts, rather than in common law negligence. Always consider whether the person suffering loss/injury was a visitor or a trespasser at the time of the accident and in the specific part of the premises on which the accident occurred. Occupiers' liability is a specialised aspect of common law negligence, and so it is relevant to consider the concepts of causation and remoteness of damages as they would apply to mainstream negligence claims where they are in issue.

Skeleton Solution

Explain and identify who is the 'occupier' of the premises concerned – discuss whether Lucille is a visitor or trespasser when she enters the garden workshop – identify the relevant Occupiers' Liability Act – discuss whether the occupier owed Lucille a duty of care, and if so, whether such a duty was broken – are Lucille's injuries too remote to recover damages for as against the occupier?

Suggested Solution

The question concerns the liability of an occupier of premises for damage done to those who come onto the premises. The law relating to such liability is largely to be found in the

Occupiers' Liability Act (OLA) 1957 as regards visitors, and the Occupiers' Liability Act (OLA) 1984 as regards non-visitors, ie trespassers.

The occupier of the premises
It is vital in all cases to correctly identify the occupier, as it is against this person or persons that a claim for loss/damage arises. Under s1(2) OLA 1957 and s1(2) OLA 1984 the definition of 'occupier' remains the same as at common law. The current test is to be found in the judgement of Lord Denning in the House of Lords case *Wheat v E Lacon and Co Ltd* (1) which defines the occupier as a person who 'has a sufficient degree of control over premises that he ought to realise that any failure on his part to use care may result in injury.'

In this case it is clear that the Browns are the occupiers of the premises, as it is they who exercise sufficient control over the garden workshop in which the accident occurred. Veronique, as an au pair, cannot be said to be an occupier of either the garden workshop or the whole house, although it is possible that she has the necessary degree of control to be regarded as the occupier of her own room.

Is Lucille a visitor or trespasser when she enters the garden workshop?
It is necessary to decide whether Lucille enters the garden workshop as visitor or non-visitor in relation to the Browns in order to determine which Occupiers' Liability Act to apply to her circumstances. This is important, because the existence and scope of any duty owed by the occupier varies according to the status of the person who comes onto the premises.

Section 1(2) OLA 1957 states that a lawful visitor is, for the purposes of the Act, either an invitee or a licensee. This requires such a person to have had the occupier's express or implied permission to come onto the premises. On the other hand, the term 'trespasser' was defined by Lord Dunedin in *Addie (Robert) and Sons (Collieries) Ltd v Dumbreck* (2) as a person 'who goes onto the land without invitation of any sort and whose presence is either unknown to the proprietor or, if known, is practically objected to.'

It is clear that Lucille lacks the Browns' express permission to enter the garden workshop, the invitation coming instead from Veronique. The question as to whether Lucille had the Browns' implied permission to enter seems to depend upon whether Veronique, as the au pair, had the Browns' actual or apparent (ostensible) authority to invite a private guest into the workshop in their absence. On this point, see *Ferguson v Welsh* (3), an analogous case on multiple occupation in which the majority of the House of Lords held that a contractor licensed to enter the occupier's premises to do work was clothed with ostensible authority to invite a subcontractor and their employees onto the land.

Ultimately, each case turns on its particular facts; however, it seems reasonable to expect that Veronique may have been permitted to receive guests in the house, but highly unlikely that such permission would have extended to a search in the workshop for spare parts to a motor scooter. Such an activity surely would have required Mr Brown's express permission. It is therefore submitted that Lucille was a trespasser when she entered the garden workshop, and that any duty owed to her by the Browns would be defined according to the requirements of OLA 1984.

Law of Tort – June 1999

Did the Browns owe Lucille a duty of care under OLA 1984 and, if so, was such a duty broken?

Under s1(3) OLA 1984 the occupier will owe the non-visitor a duty of care provided the following apply.

1. He is aware of the danger or has reasonable grounds to believe it exists. Provided, as seems likely, that Mr Brown was aware of the oil spillage, it follows that at the very least, he must have had reasonable grounds to believe that someone might slip and fall over.
2. He knows or has reasonable grounds to believe that the other (Lucille) is in the vicinity of the danger concerned, or that he may come into the vicinity of the danger (in either case, whether the other has lawful authority for being in that vicinity or not). This requirement is clearly much more difficult to satisfy in the circumstances described, as there is nothing to suggest that Mr Brown might have anticipated that anyone would enter the workshop other than himself. However, it might be argued that if Mr Brown knows that Veronique is to receive a private guest with an interest in mechanics, he might reasonably infer that the guest might be tempted to take a look in the workshop.
3. The risk is one against which, in all the circumstances of the case, he may reasonably be expected to offer the other some protection. A substantial spillage of oil could reasonably be expected to be cleaned up, or alternatively, the door to the garden workshop might easily have been locked (if applicable) and the key removed. These observations also support the argument that, provided a duty is owed by the Browns to Lucille, the duty has been broken. Section 1(4) OLA 1984 provides that the duty is 'to take such care as is reasonable in all the circumstances of the case to see that [the non-visitor] does not suffer injury on the premises by reason of the danger concerned.'

Lucille's main problem will be in establishing that a duty of care is owed to her under OLA 1984, particularly under part (2) of the three part-test above.

Assuming the Browns are in breach of a duty of care owed under OLA 1984 can they be said to have caused the loss suffered by Lucille, namely the amputated arm and the serious injuries to her leg?

Provided that Lucille satisfies the requirements of OLA 1984, she will be able to recover damages for personal injury (s1(9) OLA 1984), but not in respect of loss or damage to property; eg ripped or oil-stained clothing: s1(8) OLA 1984.

It is well established that injury to the person resulting from a breach of duty is recoverable in tort. This remains the position, even though the extent of the damage and the precise manner of its occurrence may not have been foreseeable: *Hughes v Lord Advocate* (4). Physical injury is entirely foreseeable where surfaces are slippery, and Lucille will be able to recover compensation for the loss of her arm.

The final question is whether Lucille could claim against the Browns for the injuries to her leg. A defendant is not liable unless the claimant's loss has been caused by the negligence of the defendant, both in fact and in law. The injuries to Lucille's leg have resulted, albeit indirectly, from the original injury to her arm: 'but for' the accident in the workshop, Lucille would not have been in Veronique's car when the second accident occurred: *Barnett v Chelsea and Kensington Hospital Management Committee* (5). However, it is suggested that Giles' negligent driving amounts to a new and independent intervening act by a third party (novus actus interveniens), making the leg injury too remote a consequence of any breach of OLA 1984 on the part of the Browns. In other words, it was the act of a third party (Giles) which was the true cause of the injury subsequently suffered by Lucille, an event which was completely independent of the defendant's negligence. In the words of Lord Wright in *The Oropesa* (6) the second accident was 'a new cause which disturbs the sequence of events, something which can be described as either unreasonable or extraneous or extrinsic.'

References

(1) [1966] AC 552
(2) [1929] AC 358
(3) [1987] 3 All ER 777
(4) [1963] AC 837
(5) [1969] 1 QB 428
(6) [1943] P 32

Question Six

The (fictitious) Industrial Premises (Alcohol Restriction) Regulations 1999 provide: 'No alcoholic substance shall be taken into or consumed within any premises to which these regulations apply.' The regulations apply to the premises of Goat & Sheep Ltd. Alf, who works at Goat & Sheep, buys four bottles of wine at lunchtime, brings them back to work and places them in a bag on top of the cabinet in the recreation room. During the lunch break, Bill and Clive, who also work at Goat & Sheep, and Des, a lorry driver who has been delivering supplies there, are sitting in the recreation room throwing a frisbee to each other. When Bill throws the frisbee, it strikes the bag containing the wine bottles. They are shattered; broken glass falls on Clive and Des, who are cut, and each of them loses an eye.

Advise Clive and Des.

Suggested Solution

General Comment

This is a question which required candidates to sift through a number of possible claims in tort arising from the facts, and to concentrate on those which showed the most promise. Note that the balance of the discussion should have related to breach of statutory duty rather than common law negligence.

Skeleton Solution

Breach of statutory duty – discuss whether the regulations might allow for the bringing of private civil actions in tort, either expressly or by presumption – examine the elements of a breach of statutory duty – identity of the defendant? – was a duty owed to the claimants? – were the injuries suffered of a type contemplated by the regulations? – did any breach of duty cause the damage complained of? – were Goat & Sheep Ltd vicariously liability for breach of statutory duty (if duty imposed only upon employees)? – liability in negligence – did Bill owe Clive and Des a duty of care, and if so, was it broken? – were Clive and Des contributory negligent? – was Alf negligent in leaving the bottles on top of the cabinet? – were Goat & Sheep Ltd vicariously liable for any negligence on the part of Alf or Bill? – employer's liability of Goat & Sheep Ltd?

Suggested Solution

Breach of statutory duty

The first issue to be decided in this question is whether a possible breach of the duty contained in the Industrial Premises (Alcohol Restriction) Regulations 1999 can give rise to private civil actions for breach of statutory duty in respect of the injuries suffered by Clive and Des. Such an action might lie against Goat & Sheep Ltd or Alf, depending upon whether the duty is imposed upon employers or employees. If a duty falls upon employees, there is the further question of whether Goat & Sheep Ltd can be vicariously liable for the breach of statutory duty of one of its employees.

Does an action for breach of statutory duty lie at all?
One possibility is that the regulations may expressly state whether or not civil liability will arise from their breach. If civil claims are possible, then it will be necessary to apply the elements of the tort. If not, then no action for breach of statutory duty will be possible.

If the regulations make no mention of the possibility of civil actions, then the court will have to determine whether, on their true construction, they were intended to confer a right of action in tort upon the claimant for their breach. The general rule was laid down by the House of Lords in *Lonrho Ltd v Shell Petroleum Co Ltd (No 2)* (1). Where the legislation creates an obligation and a specified means for enforcing performance of that obligation, for example by criminal penalty, there is an initial presumption that performance cannot be enforced in any other way. However, as an exception to this general rule, the courts will presume a right of action for breach of statutory duty where an obligation has been imposed for the benefit of a class of people, such as employees. Such a right may be held to exist even if the legislation does provide for criminal penalties in the event of breach: *Groves v Lord Wimborne* (2).

The Industrial Premises (Alcohol Restriction) Regulations 1999 are clearly designed to provide safety in employment and thus intended to benefit employees as a class of people. Even if the regulations do not expressly confer a right to bring a civil claim for their breach, there will certainly be a presumption to this effect.

Elements of breach of statutory duty: identity of the defendant
It is unclear from the brief quote from the regulations as to whether the duty is imposed upon employers (to prevent employees from bringing alcohol on to industrial premises and consuming it there) or upon employees, or both. This of course is a matter of interpretation. If the duty falls wholly upon employees, then an action for breach of statutory duty lies against Alf only. If, on the other hand, the duty falls wholly or partly upon employers, then Goat & Sheep Ltd are potentially liable.

Duty must be owed to the claimant
Assuming that the duty does fall upon employers, it seems likely that the regulations may only have been passed to benefit employees. Des is not an employee of Goat & Sheep Ltd. As such, only Clive would be able to claim in respect of a breach of the regulations. A similar result was arrived at by the court in *Hartley v Mayoh & Co* (3) in which a fireman's widow was unable to claim for breach of statutory duty against the defendant, in whose factory her husband had been killed, because the regulations concerned only conferred a duty upon 'persons employed'.

Injury must be of a kind which the legislation is intended to preven: Gorris *v* Scott *(4)*
A further problem arises in respect of the manner in which Clive and Des' injuries occurred. It seems likely that the regulations were intended to prevent injuries sustained in the

workplace caused by employees under the influence of alcohol, and not by accidents caused by the smashing of unattended bottles in incidents such as the one described. Clearly, the injuries suffered by Clive and Des would have been identical whether or not the bottles left on top of the cabinet contained alcohol. It is submitted that Clive and Des' injuries may therefore be of a type which these regulations were not intended to prevent. Such was the case in *Nicholls v Austin (F) (Leyton) Ltd* (5) in which a workman was unable to claim for breach of statutory duty under the Factories Act 1961 for injuries sustained when a component flew out of a machine whilst in use. The requirement that the machinery should be securely fenced was intended to prevent the workers from making contact with the machine and not vice versa.

However, Winfield and Jolowicz (6) point out that the modern approach is not to apply this requirement too strictly, and that if the damage suffered by the claimant was of the kind that the regulations were designed to prevent, then it does not matter that the precise method by which the injuries occurred was not contemplated by the legislation. Such an approach would be consistent with the decision of the House of Lords in *Hughes v Lord Advocate* (7).

A breach of the legislation has caused the damage complained of
The duty is framed in absolute terms: 'no alcoholic substance shall be taken into' and therefore Alf's action in leaving the bag containing the wine in the recreation room appears to give rise to a breach of duty. The breach has certainly caused Clive and Des' injuries in fact, and it has already been pointed out above that according to *Hughes*, the injuries are unlikely to be regarded as too remote to recover for. However, it might be argued that the conduct of the claimants, Clive and Des, in playing frisbee in the recreation room was so unreasonable as to amount to a novus actus interveniens, breaking the chain of causation: *McKew v Holland & Hannen & Cubitts (Scotland) Ltd* (8). It is more likely, however, that Clive and Des will be regarded as partly at fault for their loss, and that any damages awarded will be reduced according to an apportionment of blame under the Law Reform (Contributory Negligence) Act 1945.

Vicarious liability
If the regulations are construed as imposing duties upon employees, then the question arises as to whether Goat & Sheep Ltd could be held vicariously liable for Alf's breach of statutory duty. It has never been positively decided whether vicarious liability could exist in these circumstances, and the better approach may be for the courts to decide that a duty is imposed upon both employer and employee by the regulations. A major problem in the establishment of vicarious liability in this case is whether Alf can really be said to have been acting in the course of his employment when he brought alcohol onto Goat & Sheep Ltd's premises for his own purposes.

Negligence

Liability of Bill

It must first be considered whether Bill owes a duty of care to Clive and Des. The three part test to determine whether such a duty exists was most recently stated in *Caparo Industries Ltd plc v Dickman* (9). The first requirement is that the injuries suffered by the claimant must have been reasonably foreseeable, secondly that a close relationship of proximity existed between Bill and the claimants, and finally that it should be fair, just and reasonable in all the circumstances for the courts to impose a duty. It is arguable that a reasonable person would have foreseen some form of injury resulting from the throwing of a frisbee in an enclosed space, especially with glass or loose objects in the vicinity (although the wine bottles were concealed in a bag). The courts will readily hold that a relationship of proximity is present where physical injury has been sustained by the claimant, and it is relevant that a pre-existing relationship exists between the parties here. The most difficult element to satisfy in these circumstances is likely to be the fair, just and reasonable element of the duty test, although it is submitted that there are no specific policy considerations why Clive and Des should be denied a claim.

As to whether Bill's conduct fell below the standards to be expected of the reasonable person, it is submitted that the decision to participate indoors in an outdoor activity is in itself likely to give rise to a breach of duty to take reasonable care. It cannot be said that the risk of harm being inflicted is so unlikely that that no breach has taken place: *Bolton v Stone* (10).

No issues of causation appear to arise here. However, it is almost certainly the case that Clive and Des' voluntary involvement in the game will be regarded as a partial cause of the injuries they have suffered, and that any damages awarded will be reduced 'to such extent as the court thinks just and equitable having regard to the claimant's share in the responsibility for the damage': s1(1) Law Reform (Contributory Negligence) Act 1945. It will be for Bill to prove that Clive and Des' injuries resulted from a risk which their own fault or negligence exposed them to, and that this negligence contributed towards their injuries. It is submitted that the observations above relating to the existence of Bill's own breach of duty apply equally to Clive and Des, and that a court would probably regard them as being equally responsible for the injuries they suffered.

Once again, it is highly unlikely that Bill could be regarded as acting in the course of his employment at the time of this accident, and so Goat & Sheep Ltd are unlikely to be held vicariously liable for his negligence.

Liability of Alf

It is just possible that Alf might have been negligent in leaving the bottles on top of the cabinet, especially with seating in the vicinity. However, liability is much less likely to arise in Alf's case for the following reasons.

1. A duty of care is less likely to exist in that injuries to those in the recreation room are less foreseeable in the circumstances – unless Alf is aware that people play frisbee there, or the bottles are left in such a position that they might easily be knocked off the cabinet causing injury. It is also less likely that a court would think it fair, just and reasonable to impose a duty.

2. Novus actus interveniens arising from the independent and unreasonable actions of the claimants in playing frisbee indoors is more likely to be relevant here, breaking the chain of causation and relieving Alf of liability for Clive and Des' injuries.
3. Once again, Goat & Sheep Ltd are unlikely to be held vicariously liable for any negligence on the part of Alf. The leaving of the bottles of wine in the recreation room could hardly be described as taking place in the course of Alf's employment.

Employers' liability of Goat & Sheep Ltd

Whilst employers owe certain non-delegable duties to their staff, such as the duty to provide competent fellow employees and a safe system of working, it is submitted that it is highly unlikely that Goat & Sheep Ltd could be in breach of any of these requirements as they are, no doubt, unaware of their employees activities in the recreation room.

References

(1)   [1982] AC 173
(2)   [1898] 2 QB 402
(3)   [1954] 1 QB 383
(4)   (1874) LR 9 Exch 125
(5)   [1946] AC 493
(6)   Winfield and Jolowicz, *Tort* (15th edn, 1998) at p261
(7)   [1963] AC 837
(8)   [1969] 3 All ER 1621
(9)   [1990] 2 AC 605
(10) [1951] AC 850

Question Seven

Gina is a qualified word processor who is registered with Paperjam, a word processing agency. She is at present working at Macro & Merge Ltd, who have recruited her through Paperjam to cover for a member of staff on sick leave. On returning from lunch one day, she saw a man, whom she did not know, alone in the office loading computers onto a trolley. She struck him in the stomach, winding him and ran out locking the office door. The man was Hugo, who was employed by the maintenance department of Macro & Merge, and he was removing the computers in the course of his work. Hugo was known to his employers to suffer from asthma and to be prone to blackouts during which he sometimes needed assistance. Hugo had a very severe asthmatic attack and passed out. He has suffered permanent damage to his health.

Advise Hugo as to any claims in tort.

Suggested Solution

General Comment

This ought to have been a relatively straightforward question for those candidates who were familiar with the torts of trespass to the person. In addition, it is always necessary to consider the possibility of employer's liability in negligence where injuries are sustained by an employee in the course of employment.

Skeleton Solution

Discuss Gina's liability for claims in battery and false imprisonment – are Hugo's injuries too remote given his unusual physical susceptibility? – examine the defences of lawful arrest to a claim of false imprisonment and self-defence to a claim in battery – if Gina has committed a tort against Hugo, are either Macro & Merge Ltd or Paperjam vicariously liable? – who was Gina employed by? – was her attack in the course of her employment? – are Macro & Merge Ltd liable in negligence on the basis of a breach of the duty to provide a safe system of work? – were Hugo's injuries too remote to recover for, given his unusual physical susceptibility?

Suggested Solution

Claims against Gina

Gina's liability in tort is relatively easy to establish in these circumstances. Hugo may have claims in battery and false imprisonment.

Law of Tort – June 1999

Battery
Battery is the intentional and direct application of unlawful force to another. The elements of battery are easily satisfied in this case. The contact with Hugo's stomach was a direct act on the part of Gina, ie a direct cause of her act of striking him. The act itself was intentional rather than merely accidental or negligent: *Letang v Cooper* (1). The force used by Gina is certainly likely to be regarded as unlawful in that it was either hostile in the circumstances: *Wilson v Pringle* (2) or without lawful excuse, lacking Hugo's consent: *Re F (Mental Patient: Sterilisation)* (3). Battery, along with other trespass related torts, is actionable per se, without the need to prove any injury to the claimant.

False imprisonment
This is the infliction of bodily restraint which is not expressly or impliedly authorised by law. Once again, the elements of false imprisonment appear to be present in the circumstances described. The confinement of the claimant must be such that his liberty is totally restrained: *Bird v Jones* (4) with no reasonable means of escape. An issue here is whether Hugo was aware of his apparent confinement to the office after Gina's attack. Early authority appeared to suggest that false imprisonment is not committed where the claimant is unaware of any restriction placed upon his freedom: *Herring v Boyle* (5). The modern approach, however, seems to be that a person can be falsely imprisoned whilst unconscious, although any award of damages will be purely nominal unless the claimant suffers some other form of harm as a result: *Murray v Ministry of Defence* (6). It is submitted that Gina's intentional locking of the office door almost certainly gives rise to a claim for false imprisonment, and that Hugo is likely to be entitled to compensatory damages for any period of awareness of his confinement before he passed out, and possibly after he came to, and the fact that the harm he suffered following Gina's attack was aggravated by his on-going confinement without medical treatment.

Remoteness
Battery and false imprisonment are trespasses against the person, and as such are actionable per se without the need to prove any injury to the claimant. This means that Hugo can recover for all the injuries resulting from Gina's unlawful acts, whether or not they were foreseeable, including any direct harm caused by the impact to his stomach, the suffering caused by the winding and the subsequent asthma attack, and the injuries resulting in permanent damage to Hugo's health.

Defences
The main defence to a claim of false imprisonment is lawful arrest. Section 24(4) Police and Criminal Evidence Act 1984 allows anyone, including a private citizen, to make an arrest where they have reasonable grounds for suspecting that an arrestable offence is being committed (even if, in fact, there is no offence). It will be for Gina to justify any arrest on the balance of probabilities, unless she is to be found liable for false imprisonment. She will have to establish that she actually believed Hugo was in the course of committing a theft (an arrestable offence), and further, that she had reasonable grounds to suspect that he was doing so. It is this latter aspect which may cause problems for Gina. It could be argued that an objective observer would take the view that Gina's initial suspicion did not turn into a reasonable one, because she failed to challenge Hugo as to his presence in the office and to

ask to see some identification. Macro & Merge Ltd appear to be a large employer, and Gina as a temporary member of staff clearly cannot expect to recognise everyone in the office. However, the question of reasonable suspicion is one which will have to be determined in all the circumstances of the case.

There is a further question as to the lawfulness of any arrest carried out by Gina, in that the provision of some information to the suspect upon arrest is normally necessary, unless the fact and grounds for arrest are obvious: *Christie* v *Leachinsky* (7). In other cases, probably such as this, Gina would be required to give sufficient information to inform Hugo as to the factual and legal basis of the accusation against him. In the absence of such an explanation, there will be no valid lawful arrest.

It is unlikely that Gina will be able to raise self-defence to a claim of battery against Hugo. Gina would effectively have to establish the existence of a defence in tort of 'mistaken self-defence of the property of another', requiring considerable expansion of the existing authorities in this area.

Claims against Macro & Merge Ltd and Paperjam

Vicarious liability
Whilst Gina's liability in tort appears to be easily established, Hugo will want to claim against an organisation which is better placed to compensate him than a temporary employee. Gina's employer will almost certainly carry an insurance policy to meet such a claim. The two main issues that arise here relate to the identity of Gina's employer at the time of the incident and whether Gina was acting in the course of her employment when she attacked Hugo.

Who is the employer?
It is unclear whether Gina is employed on a temporary basis by Macro & Merge Ltd, or on an on-going basis by the agency that supplied her. The modern approach is for the courts to consider a range of factors and to examine all the circumstances of Gina's working relationship as against each potential employer. Such factors, none of which are conclusive on their own, will include the following.

1. Who paid Gina's wages and National Insurance contributions in return for her work and skill?
2. Who had the authority to exercise a sufficient degree of control over the manner in which Gina did her work?
3. Who could dismiss Gina?
4. How long was she hired out for?

Was Gina in the course of her employment when she attacked Hugo?
Assuming, for a moment, that Gina is an employee of Macro & Merge Ltd, she will be impliedly authorised (although not legally bound) to protect her employer's property, provided that her actions are not so outrageous that a reasonable employer would not have contemplated them as being within the scope of employment. For example, an employee was held to be acting in the course of his employment when he struck a boy whom he reasonably believed to be in the course of steeling goods belonging to his employer: *Polland*

v *Parr & Sons* (8). If the employee acts so excessively beyond what is necessary to deal with the emergency (eg were Gina to have shot Hugo) then the employee steps beyond the scope of his employment.

It is submitted, on this basis, that Gina is acting in the course of her employment with Macro & Merge Ltd. However, it may be one stage too far removed to suggest that she is acting in the course of any employment with Paperjam, the agency which supplied her, when acting to protect Macro & Merge Ltd's property against what she assumed was a theft.

Employers' liability

Macro & Merge Ltd may be liable in negligence for a breach of their non-delegable duty to devise and operate a safe system of work. Such a duty may arise in view of their knowledge of Hugo's asthmatic condition, his susceptibility to blackouts and his subsequent need for occasional assistance. The particular characteristics of a claimant are relevant in deciding how a reasonable employer ought to have discharged its duty. In *Paris v Stepney Borough Council* (9) for example, an employer's failure to provide an employee, who was already blind in one eye, with safety goggles amounted to a breach of this duty due to the serious possible (and actual) consequences of the employee sustaining further eye injury. Thus it could be argued that Macro & Merge Ltd's failure to ensure that Hugo was accompanied at all times by another member of staff amounts to a breach of the duty to provide a safe system of work. Clearly, injury to Hugo was foreseeable as a result of the failure to provide adequate supervision, and so it does not matter that the extent of Hugo's injuries, and the precise way in which they occurred, could not have been foreseen: *Hughes v Lord Advocate* (10).

References

(1) [1965] 1 QB 232
(2) [1987] QB 237
(3) [1990] 2 AC 1
(4) (1845) 7 QB 742
(5) (1834) 1 Cr M & R 377
(6) [1988] 2 All ER 521
(7) [1947] AC 573
(8) [1927] 1 KB 236
(9) [1951] AC 367
(10) [1963] AC 837

Question Eight

Ronald leased a small country house from Percival. With Percival's consent, he assigned the unexpired two years of the lease to Stewart in 1998. A shed in the garden contained a considerable amount of rubbish including some paint tins. Stewart did not want to use the shed, did not ask Ronald to remove the rubbish and did not investigate what was there. The paint tins had in fact been used to store a highly corrosive chemical. It has now destroyed the containers and seeped into the adjoining property of Terence. It has made it impossible to grow flowers in a large part of Terence's garden and has destroyed his prize sunflowers. Stewart has disposed of the paint tins but says that he cannot do anything about the chemical which has seeped into the soil. Terence knows that Stewart always likes to watch the 'Newsnight' programme at 10.30 each evening on television and Terence always uses electrical equipment at the time in order to interfere with reception. Ronald's present whereabouts are unknown.

Advise the parties.

Suggested Solution

General Comment

Students who were well aware of the recent House of Lords decisions in *Hunter* v *Canary Wharf* and to a lesser extent *Cambridge Water* would have been well placed to answer this question. A thorough knowledge of the rules would have been necessary to have made some observations on the question of whether Percival might be liable to Terence in respect of the escaped chemicals.

Skeleton Solution

Terence – action in private nuisance for the escaped chemicals – does Terence have sufficient standing to bring a claim? – can a single event give rise to liability in private nuisance? – who can Terence sue? – measure of damages – alternative action in *Rylands* v *Fletcher* – whether the storage of the chemicals was a non-natural use of the land – who can Terence sue? – Stewart – whether interference with TV reception can form the basis of an action in private nuisance – whether nuisance is actionable (noting the relevance of malice) – brief mention of remedies.

Law of Tort – June 1999

Suggested Solution

Damages for the clean up costs of Terence's land and the destroyed flowers are potentially recoverable in both the tort of private nuisance and under the rule in *Rylands v Fletcher* (1).

Private nuisance

Private nuisance has been defined by Winfield and Jolowicz as 'an unlawful interference with a person's use or enjoyment of land, or some right over, or in connection with it.' The House of Lords in *Hunter v Canary Wharf Ltd* (2) confirmed that private nuisance is a tort which attaches to land, and so only those with a proprietorial interest in the land affected may bring an action. Terence must therefore be a freeholder, a tenant in possession or a licensee with exclusive possession of the neighbouring premises in order to have sufficient standing to bring a claim.

Generally, nuisances may take three different forms: encroachment on a neighbour's land, direct physical injury to a neighbour's land or interference with a neighbour's quiet enjoyment of the land. Whilst Terence's land has suffered direct physical damage, there is some uncertainty as to whether an isolated or a single escape can constitute a nuisance. The position appears to be that if damage resulted from a pre-existing state of affairs, it will constitute a nuisance: see *Midwood v Manchester Corportation* (3) in which a gas explosion was held to be an actionable nuisance as it followed a build-up of gas in the main. It is clearly arguable that the migrating chemical which caused damage to Terence's land resulted from their storage and gradual escape from the shed next door over a period of time, and it is therefore submitted that this amounted to a pre-existing state of affairs giving rise to a nuisance.

Who can Terence sue?

Ronald's whereabouts are unknown and so Terence's potential claims are against Percival (the reversioner) and Stewart (the tenant). It is not clear whether it was Ronald or Percival who accumulated the paint tins. Stewart was not responsible for their presence. If Percival was responsible for the storage of the chemical, he may be held liable as a previous occupier of the premises, because he knew, or ought to have known, of the hazardous state of affairs: *St Anne's Well Brewery Co v Roberts* (4).

As for Stewart, there is authority to suggest that he will be liable as an occupying tenant of the premises: *Montana Hotels v Fasson Pty* (5). Stewart's liability, notwithstanding his ignorance of the hazard, would seem to be consistent with the notion of strict liability in the tort of private nuisance.

Was this an actionable nuisance?

In determining whether the nuisance is actionable, the courts balance the reasonableness of the defendant's activity (which created the nuisance) against the reasonable needs of the claimant to use and enjoy his property. However, in *St Helens Smelting Co v Tipping* (6), the House of Lords held that there was a distinction between nuisances which cause damage to property and those which cause personal discomfort in the use or enjoyment of land. It is easier to establish nuisance in the former case, as the courts do not take into account the character of the area as a relevant factor. We have already seen that single escapes of the type which occurred in this case can amount to actionable nuisances, and it is submitted that the fact of physical damage to Terence's land in the circumstances will allow him to claim. There appear to be no problems as to whether damage of the kind that took place in this case was foreseeable, given the highly corrosive nature of the chemical being stored: *Cambridge Water Company* v *Eastern Counties Leather plc* (7).

Damages
Terence will be able to claim compensation according to the diminution in value of his land. This is likely to be equal to the cost of re-instatement, ie the clean up costs. Terence ought to be able to claim, in addition, compensation for the cost of the plants and flowers destroyed. There seems to be no English authority on the question of whether Terence could claim for any economic losses flowing from prizes he might have won in respect of the sunflowers.

Rylands *v* Fletcher
Since the *Cambridge Water* case, it is clear that this tort is nothing more than a specific application of the law of private nuisance in relation to isolated escapes. For liability to attach under this rule, it must be proved that:

1. the defendant brought something onto his land in the course of some non-natural use of it;
2. there has been an escape of that thing from the defendant's land to the claimant's land;
3. damage has resulted to the claimant's property; and
4. it must have been foreseeable that damage of the kind that took place would occur.

The only issue here is whether the corrosive chemical amounted to a non-natural use of the land. This concept receives no precise definition in the authorities, although Lord Goff in the *Cambridge Water* case stated: 'The storage of substantial quantities of chemicals on industrial premises should be regarded as an almost classic case of non-natural use.' Whether the storage of some paint tins containing a highly corrosive chemical on residential premises would be regarded as a non-natural use is uncertain. It might be argued that if the storage of chemicals is a non-natural use of industrial premises, it certainly ought to be so regarded on residential premises, even if the quantities involved are less. In general, the more dangerous a thing is, the more likely it is to constitute a non-natural use.

Who can Terence sue?
In *Rylands* v *Fletcher* Blackburn J spoke of a person who 'for his own purposes' brings things onto his land. This would appear to rule out Stewart as a potential defendant, liability thus depending upon whether it was Percival or Ronald who was responsible for the storage of the paint tins. However, in *Cambridge Water*, the rule in *Rylands* v *Fletcher* was held to be an offshoot of the tort of private nuisance. In view of this, it is might be argued that the same rules should apply in relation to potential defendants as were discussed for private nuisance.

Is Terence liable to Stewart for the interference with TV reception?
Stewart, as a tenant, has a proprietorial interest in the land affected by Terence's activities and therefore has sufficient standing to mount an action in private nuisance. The first issue is whether interference with TV reception can amount to a private nuisance. Comments

made by Buckley J in the case of *Bridlington Relay Ltd v Yorkshire Electricity Board* (8) suggested that, at the time of that case, TV reception could not be regarded as such an important part of an ordinary householder's enjoyment of his property so as to amount to a legal nuisance. However, more recent cases in other common law jurisdictions have held that TV viewing is an important incident of the ordinary enjoyment of property and should be protected. In *Hunter*, the House of Lords held that interference with TV reception caused by the blocking of such transmissions by the erection of a building did not constitute a nuisance. However, obiter comments of Lords Hoffman and Cooke suggest that interference with TV reception could, in some circumstances, amount to a nuisance. In the light of the decision in *Hunter*, it is submitted that where such interference is caused by something emanating from the defendant's land, such as Terence's use of electrical equipment, then an action will lie. The point remains to be firmly decided.

Assuming that such interference can form the basis of a claim in nuisance, it must be decided according to the balancing test whether or not there is an actionable nuisance. All the factors in this case point to the resolution of that balancing exercise in favour of Stewart. In the normal course of events, relevant factors would be as follows.

1. The character of the neighbourhood in which the nuisance took place. The facts of the question indicate a residential countryside area, where interference with TV reception is likely to be uncommon and therefore subjectively more disturbing.
2. The fact that the interference took place at night time, when residents are most likely to be viewing TV.
3. The fact that this was a repeated and continuing interference.

Moreover, the fact that Terence was motivated by malice tips the balance very firmly in Stewart's favour (*Christie v Davey* (9)) and it is submitted that the court is likely to be persuaded to grant an injunction restraining or restricting Terence's use of the electrical equipment. Stewart may also be entitled to damages for the loss of amenity value to his property covering the period of intentional interference up to the time of any injunction. Any such award would consist of a relatively low one-off payment.

References

(1) (1868) LR 3 HL 330
(2) [1997] 2 All ER 426
(3) [1905] 2 KB 597
(4) (1928) 140 LT 1
(5) (1986) 69 ALR 258
(6) (1865) 11 HL Cas 642
(7) [1994] 2 WLR 53
(8) [1965] Ch 436
(9) [1893] 1 Ch 316

Suggested Solutions to Past Examination Questions 1998–1999

The Suggested Solutions series provides examples of full answers to the questions regularly set by examiners. Each suggested solution has been broken down into three stages: general comment, skeleton solution and suggested solution. The examination questions included within the text are taken from past examination papers set by the London University. The full opinion answers will undoubtedly assist you with your research and further your understanding and appreciation of the subject in question.

Only £6.95 Published January 2001

Constitutional Law
ISBN: 1 85836 389 6

Contract Law
ISBN: 1 85836 390 X

Criminal Law
ISBN: 1 85836 391 8

English Legal System
ISBN: 1 85836 392 6

Jurisprudence and Legal Theory
ISBN: 1 85836 393 4

Land Law
ISBN: 1 85836 394 2

Law of Tort
ISBN: 1 85836 395 0

Law of Trusts
ISBN: 1 85836 396 9

Forthcoming titles of Suggested Solutions 1999–2000 due January 2002

Company Law
ISBN: 1 85836 442 6

European Union Law
ISBN: 1 85836 443 4

Evidence
ISBN: 1 85836 444 2

Family Law
ISBN: 1 85836 445 0

Public International Law
ISBN: 1 85836 446 9

For further information on contents or to place an order, please contact:
Mail Order
Old Bailey Press
200 Greyhound Road
London
W14 9RY

Telephone No: 020 7381 7407
Fax No: 020 7386 0952
Website: www.oldbaileypress.co.uk

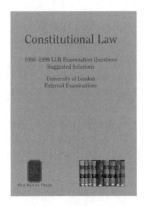

Old Bailey Press

The Old Bailey Press integrated student law library is tailor-made to help you at every stage of your studies from the preliminaries of each subject through to the final examination. The series of Textbooks, Revision WorkBooks, 150 Leading Cases/Casebooks and Cracknell's Statutes are interrelated to provide you with a comprehensive set of study materials.

You can buy Old Bailey Press books from your University Bookshop, your local Bookshop, direct using this form, or you can order a free catalogue of our titles from the address shown overleaf.

The following subjects each have a Textbook, 150 Leading Cases/Casebook, Revision WorkBook and Cracknell's Statutes unless otherwise stated.

Administrative Law
Commercial Law
Company Law
Conflict of Laws
Constitutional Law
Conveyancing (Textbook and Casebook)
Criminal Law
Criminology (Textbook and Sourcebook)
English and European Legal Systems
Equity and Trusts
Evidence
Family Law
Jurisprudence: The Philosophy of Law (Textbook, Sourcebook and
    Revision WorkBook)
Land: The Law of Real Property
Law of International Trade
Law of the European Union
Legal Skills and System
Obligations: Contract Law
Obligations: The Law of Tort
Public International Law
Revenue Law (Textbook,
    Sourcebook and Revision
    WorkBook)
Succession

Mail order prices:	
Textbook	£14.95
150 Leading Cases/Casebook	£9.95
Revision WorkBook	£7.95
Cracknell's Statutes	£9.95
Suggested Solutions 1998–1999	£6.95
Law Update 2001	£9.95

To complete your order, please fill in the form below:

Module	Books required	Quantity	Price	Cost
		Postage		
		TOTAL		

For Europe, add 15% postage and packing (£20 maximum).
For the rest of the world, add 40% for airmail.

ORDERING

By telephone to Mail Order at 020 7381 7407, with your credit card to hand.

By fax to 020 7386 0952 (giving your credit card details).

Website: www.oldbaileypress.co.uk

By post to: Mail Order, Old Bailey Press, 200 Greyhound Road, London W14 9RY.

When ordering by post, please enclose full payment by cheque or banker's draft, or complete the credit card details below. You may also order a free catalogue of our complete range of titles from this address.

We aim to despatch your books within 3 working days of receiving your order.

Name

Address

Postcode   Telephone

Total value of order, including postage: £

I enclose a cheque/banker's draft for the above sum, or

charge my   ☐ Access/Mastercard   ☐ Visa   ☐ American Express
Card number

☐☐☐☐ ☐☐☐☐ ☐☐☐☐ ☐☐☐☐

Expiry date   ☐☐☐☐

Signature: .... Date: ....